Mexican Roots, American Schools

Helping Mexican Immigrant Children Succeed

Robert Crosnoe

Stanford University Press
Stanford, California,
2006

Stanford University Press
Stanford, California

Library of Congress Cataloging-in-Publication Data

Crosnoe, Robert.
    Mexican roots, American schools : helping Mexican immigrant children succeed / Robert Crosnoe.
        p.   cm.
    Includes bibliographical references and index.
    ISBN-13: 978-0-8047-5522-1 (cloth : alk. paper)
    ISBN-13: 978-0-8047-5523-8 (pbk : alk. paper)
        1. Mexican American children—Education (Elementary) 2. Child development—United States. 3. Mexicans—United States—Social conditions. I. Title.

LC2683.3.C76 2006
371.82968′72073—dc22
2006004579
Typeset by G&S Book Services in 10/14 Minion

Original Printing 2006
Last figure below indicates year of this printing:
15 14 13 12 11 10 09 08 07 06

Mexican Roots, American Schools

For the Crosnoes and the Cavanaghs,
especially Shannon, Joseph, and Caroline

Contents

Tables

Figures

Acknowledgments

I NEVER DO THINGS ALONE, and so anything that appears under my name can most assuredly be viewed as a group project. So, let me use a little space here to thank the various members of my group.

The Foundation for Child Development in New York supported this line of research through their Changing Faces of America Young Scholars Program. Under the guidance of Ruby Takanishi, this foundation is putting its money where its mouth is when it comes to improving the lives of America's young newcomers, and I consider myself lucky to be a part of that. Annette Chin, in particular, deserves a great big hand for helping the other young scholars and me during our work with the foundation.

Of course, this book is also a product of my training (years in the making) and my current professional environment. Consequently, I have to thank those who helped me get where I am as well as those who keep me going now that I am here. The former include Sandy Dornbusch at Stanford University and Glen Elder at the University of North Carolina at Chapel Hill, and the latter include the people at the Department of Sociology and the Population Research Center at the University of Texas at Austin, especially Chandra Muller, Bob Hummer, Deb Umberson, Aletha Huston, Kelly Raley, the PRC administrative services core, my research assistants (especially Lizy Wildsmith), and my friends and colleagues on the Adolescent Health and Academic Project. Outside the University of Texas, I also need to send regards to Ken Frank, Karl Alexander, Barbara Schneider, Don Hernandez, and the members of the NICHD Early Child Care Network for their help and support.

Finally, at the end of this list are the people who, in my life, never come last. No acknowledgment could be complete without thanking my parents, Caven and Sue Crosnoe, and my brothers and sisters: Wade, Kristen, Clark, and Aparna. I have also had the blessing to see my family expand in the last few years to include my in-laws (including a new mother, father, sisters, and brothers) and many assorted nieces and nephews. Most important, however, there are three: my children, Joseph and Caroline, who have taught me more about child development than any book ever written, and their mother, Shannon, who has taught me everything else I know to be true.

Mexican Roots, American Schools

1 American Dreams for a New Generation

THE NUMBERS CERTAINLY DO GRAB YOUR ATTENTION: 115,864, that is the number of Mexican immigrants who came to the United States in 2003; 3,100,000, that is the number of Mexican immigrants who currently have legal resident status in the United States; 55,946, that is the number of Mexican immigrants who were granted U.S. citizenship in 2003; 2,400,000, that is the number of Mexican immigrants who are currently eligible for U.S. citizenship.[1] Even presented as simple, basic statistics without context, these numbers go a long way toward capturing the future of American society—how immigration from Mexico will, in the coming years, profoundly alter, transform, diversify, and enrich everything about the United States, from its economy to its cultural fabric to the essence of what it means to be an American. At the same time, these numbers build bridges between the future and the present and the distant as well as the not-so-distant past by linking a long history, in which immigration served as a workhorse in the building of the U.S. population and as a wellspring in the continual renewal of American culture, to a tomorrow in which a new demography truly is our destiny.

What is the story hiding behind these numbers? It is doubtless one of hope, one of immeasurable expectation. Day after day, week after week, year after year, Mexicans migrate to the United States through various methods and points of entry, in search of better jobs, expanded opportunities, greater freedoms, new experiences, and things far less specific, such as hazy, ill-defined, but powerful images of a better tomorrow. In short, they come to improve their lives by making a journey that covers a relatively small geographic space but a great social and economic chasm. Importantly, they come with their children,

1

those already born and growing, those about to be born, those who will be born at some point in the future. These children, in fact, are often the primary motivation for immigration and become the receptacles of their parents' American dreams. Above and beyond their expectations of what they may gain for themselves in their new country, Mexican immigrants look to their children's futures as the true, enduring payoff of their journey and of all the trials and tribulations that this journey entails.

We know, of course, that these dreams go unrealized more often than not. Breathtakingly high poverty rates go along with low social mobility. Jobs do not materialize, and, when they do, they do not pay well or do not last. Immigrants are met with institutionalized and even legalized discrimination. They face social, economic, residential, and cultural obstacles that seem nearly impossible to surmount. A good deal of scientific research tells us so, as do many of the observations of and experiences with Mexican immigrants in our own personal lives. These unrealized dreams, however, are not a persuasive argument against the decision to immigrate, nor evidence of the necessity of closing the U.S.-Mexican border, or even a valid reason to lose hope. Instead, these dashed dreams, when coupled with the statistics described earlier, are a call to arms. The time is *now* to figure out how to facilitate the realization of the dreams at the heart of the Mexican immigrant experience.

The children of Mexican immigrant families should be a primary focal point in the pursuit of this basic but important goal. Statistics on the exponential growth of these children in the U.S. student population have generated a good deal of heated debate and often emotional rhetoric from the highest levels of policy development and implementation down to the dinner tables of individual families in towns across the nation. We have all seen the recent protests and counterprotests in the streets of the United States after all. These statistics are generally seen as a cause for concern, of alarm even. Yet the growing number of young children from Mexican immigrant families also represents an invaluable opportunity in national attempts to improve the long-term prospects of the Mexican immigrant population. Not only are these young children just beginning their life pathways, but they also stand at the threshold of a societal institution—the educational system—that wields arguably the greatest power in setting and directing these life pathways.

Consider, therefore, this sequence: (1) Improving the prospects of the Mexican immigrant population is best served by improving the educational prospects of the children in this population; (2) making such improvements must be taken up by social policy, on the large and small scale; and (3) such policy must be constructed on a solid foundation of knowledge about what helps and what hurts these children in the U.S. educational system. The goal of this study is to pick up the third step in this sequence as a means of promoting the first two steps. No less than the dreams of a population are at stake.

Immigration, Education, and Social Policy

So, children are the future and education matters. These are platitudes really, but in the case of emigration from Mexico, they pack a most powerful truth. The modern U.S. economy is often described as having a peculiarly hourglass shape, with broad strata of high-paying, stable jobs in the professions at the top, even broader strata of low-paying, insecure jobs in service and related sectors at the bottom, and little in between.[2] In this hourglass economy, educational success, especially college and advanced degrees, is crucial to pushing through the bottleneck into the high-reward strata. In this way, education is the primary "conveyer belt" to social mobility, even more so than in past historical eras.[3]

Such mobility is, undoubtedly, a gradual, long-term process, one that plays out over decades of educational and occupational experiences. Regardless of the time frame, however, it is also a process that has enduring effects on the lives of individual Mexican-origin children as well as on the basic social and economic status of the Mexican-origin population as a whole. In short, educational success is a means by which Mexican immigrant parents' dreams for their children can be fulfilled, even if their own personal social status does not improve and even if the eventual social advantages accrued by their children take a lifetime to emerge.[4]

Given the potential significance of educational success as a solution to the paradox of immigration from the United States's nearest neighbor to the south, the most pressing question, of course, becomes, How can we promote the educational success of children from Mexican immigrant families? As I have already mentioned, this goal requires social policy based on careful research detailing the successes and failures, risks and resources, and steps forward and backward of these children. The building of this crucial knowledge base is currently under way, actively constructed by sociologists, psychologists, economists, political scientists, and the like. For this general knowledge base to be specifically policy relevant, however, some fine-tuning is required.

First, we must build knowledge about the factors associated with educational success among children from Mexican immigrant families that coincide with *critical intervention points*. In other words, we need to identify tools that can be successfully leveraged at times when they are most likely to have long-term consequences. Decades of educational and developmental research have demonstrated that key life transition points, including school transitions, are such critical periods.[5] Indeed, the transition into elementary school may be an especially fruitful time to intervene because it represents the foundation of the educational career. It is the starting gate. It is where potential is still yet to be realized, when all avenues are more open than they will ever be.

Second, uncovering factors associated with educational successes and failures is always an important enterprise, but uncovering such factors that are also *policy amenable* is especially valuable. For example, consider some interpersonal factor, such as emotional support from peers, that may be closely associated with academic functioning but is also exceedingly difficult to manipulate from the outside, even more so on a national scale. Research on this factor promotes knowledge about the educational process but is not especially helpful from a policy standpoint. Conversely, other personal or contextual factors that are more amenable to policy interventions—such as health and its amenability to health services or school context and its amenability to institutional reorganization—are useful from a policy standpoint even if they are not as powerfully related to academic functioning.[6]

Third, our arsenal of scientific methods is indeed vast, and different weapons in this arsenal make their own unique contribution to the *multidimensional* enterprise of crafting empirically based social policies aimed at reducing demographic inequalities in education.[7] Qualitative, community-based methods allow the careful elucidation of specific mechanisms of inequality and the rich understanding of particular groups within context, whereas experimental and quasi-experimental methods allow the establishment of causal influences in processes of inequality. Large-scale quantitative research promotes generalizability and the investigation of contextual variability, both of which help us to figure out what interventions are needed and which ones are most likely to have the broadest impact.[8] All have their own value, and each needs to be pursued with that specific value in mind.

At the heart of this book is an empirical research study. The purpose of this study was to follow the guidelines just described to produce knowledge about the educational careers of children from Mexican immigrant families. This knowledge can then be leveraged to inform social policy that targets the long-term social and economic prospects of this exponentially growing population. It is a theoretically grounded, policy-focused study of the transition to elementary school that draws on a nationally representative sample of children, sophisticated statistical methodology, and aspects of child development that are amenable to policy intervention. In the following section I trace out the basic theoretical blueprint of this study.

Overview of the Study

In an influential monograph published by the Society for Research in Child Development in 1988, two sociologists of education, Karl Alexander and Doris Entwisle, articulated one of the most comprehensive and provocative theoretical models of the transition into and through elementary school. This school transition model, which is a foundation of the now booming field of educational research on kindergarten and first-grade entry,[9] grew out of extensive research on elementary school students from diverse backgrounds in Baltimore, Maryland. Its general premise is that the well-documented and often-discussed race, class, and other demographic disparities in educational attainment emerge out of experiences in the earliest years of schooling. Indeed, demographic differences in performance and learning are relatively narrow and highly malleable in the first two or three years of elementary school, but over time they slowly widen and eventually calcify. Consequently, to have an impact, interventions must target early differences. The school transition model was designed to shed light on the roots of these early differences. These roots have less to do with intellectual abilities than with the general circumstances of children's lives. Specifically, the model contends that children from different demographic populations enter elementary school with sharp differences in personal, experiential, and social psychological factors (e.g., personal competencies, early enrichment, interpersonal support) that translate into small differences in early learning. These small early differences compound over time as initial performance sets teacher and peer expectations, influences class assignment, and affects self-evaluations. In this way children from more disadvantaged populations lose ground to their peers until the cycle becomes self-reinforcing.[10] Thus one of the most disheartening aspects of the school transition model is also one of its most hopeful: Inequality is a long time in the making but does not have to be so.

As already mentioned, the school transition model is the blueprint of this study. Obviously, Mexican immigrant status is the aspect of social background that drives my particular application of this model. In short, I have comprehensively analyzed the linkage between Mexican immigrant status and early learn-

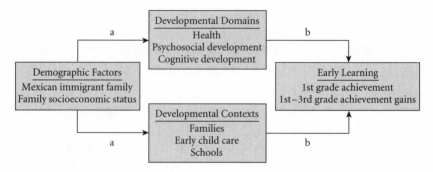

Figure 1.1 School transition model for children from Mexican immigrant families

ing in a nationally representative sample of U.S. kindergartners. This sample, the Early Childhood Longitudinal Study–Kindergarten Cohort (ECLS-K), was collected by the National Center for Education Statistics, a research wing of the federal government, precisely for the national-level investigation of policy-relevant educational issues. The ins and outs of the ECLS-K data and how I analyzed these data are described in full in Chapter 2.

Following the school transition model, the basic premise of this study is that children from Mexican immigrant families enter school with wildly different life circumstances than their peers (see Path A in Figure 1.1). These circumstances are broken down into two general categories. The first category encompasses three different domains of child development. In other words, I look within children—at their individual characteristics, abilities, and behaviors—to understand differences in early learning between children from Mexican immigrant families and their peers, specifically, their health, psychosocial development, and cognitive development (Chapter 3). The second category encompasses three different contexts of development. In other words, I look outside children—at the physical and interpersonal settings of their lives—to determine what differentiates children from Mexican immigrant families from their peers in the early years of schooling, specifically, their families, experiences in early child care, and the elementary schools that they attend (Chapter 4).

Next, I attempt to determine whether these differences in children's general development and in the contexts in which this development occurs translate into differences in early learning between children from Mexican immigrant families and their peers (see Path B in Figure 1.1). After comparing rates of learning in the first grade and then growth in learning between the first and third grades of children from Mexican immigrant families and their native White, African-American, Asian-American, and other Latino/a peers, I assess the degree to which any differences related to Mexican immigrant status are explained by concomitant differences in health, psychosocial development, cognitive development, family processes, early child care experiences, and elementary school contexts (Chapter 5). Some of these developmental and contextual factors are hypothesized to boost the relative standing of children from Mexican immigrant families; others are hypothesized to be obstacles to their school readiness and early learning. My primary task is to find out which matter, how much they matter, and in what ways they matter.

Four Issues of Note

At the start of any large-scale study, difficult decisions need to be made about how things will progress, and my particular study was no different. I had to tailor the basic blueprint in several ways that deserve further comment. These decisions allowed me to execute this research effectively while staying true to its theoretical underpinnings and its policy-related objectives.

First, this study focuses exclusively on early learning in one subject: math. The reasons for this focus are both conceptual and practical. Conceptually, math is a core curriculum of elementary school and one that, unlike reading, maintains its curricular centrality through high school and beyond. Success in math is crucial to performance on high-stakes tests, the accumulation of valued academic credentials, postsecondary matriculation, and entry into the more rewarded sectors of the hourglass economy at the end of school.[11] Practically, the Mexican-origin children in the ECLS-K were allowed to take math achievement tests (but not other kinds of achievement tests) in Spanish if they did not have good English-language proficiency. Consequently, math is the one academic arena in which their skill level can be adequately assessed independent of their language skills. Thus certain circumstances warranted a more narrow academic focus than I would have liked, but that one academic focus happens to be of the utmost importance.

Second, I have collapsed together two groups—first-generation children (those born in Mexico to Mexican-born parents) and second-generation children (those born in the United States to Mexican-born parents)—that, in adolescence-focused research, are generally examined separately.[12] Recall, however, that the focus of this study is on young children. Even at a maximum, a second-generation child could not have lived in the United States much longer than a first-generation child, and the amount of time that a first-generation child could have lived in Mexico is small. What connects them is an important commonality. Both first- and second-generation children are being raised in the United States by parents who were born in Mexico. For this reason I borrow the terminology of the Suarez-Orozcos as well as the National Academy of Sciences, leaders in research on the development of immigrant children, and refer to first- and second-generation children together as children from Mexican immigrant families.

Third, the primary concern of this study is the potential for differences in various domains and contexts of child development related to Mexican immigration to translate into corresponding differences in early learning. This focus, although broad, appears to leave out a major culprit in the creation and reinforcement of such differences, namely, the socioeconomic circumstances of the family. We know that Mexican immigrants have more negative socioeconomic circumstances—such as fewer years of schooling, lower income, less prestigious jobs—than other Americans. Moreover, I will hardly surprise the reader by stating that socioeconomic circumstances are closely related to different aspects of child development, including school adjustment and achievement.[13] Rest assured, therefore, that socioeconomic status will be taken into account in this study. More specifically, the contributions of immigrant status and family socioeconomic status will always be carefully delineated, whether looking at health, school enrollment, math learning, or anything else. Doing so allows me to assess the degree to which the "effects" of immigrant status on children's lives are channeled through their socioeconomic circumstances, which, in turn, allows more careful consideration of where intervention should be targeted.

Fourth, the conclusions drawn in this study are the product of extensive and complex quantitative analysis of an enormous data set. The statistical models estimated here and the results that they produced are indeed voluminous. In such a situation one is left with the choice of whether to comprehensively present the numbers or to draw a basic picture from these numbers and leave the actual statistics more or less in the background. I chose the latter approach. All aspects of quantitative methodology are included in the Appendix, and I have used the main chapters to tell a complicated story in a straightforward way with narrative, some tables, and illustrative figures. This approach allows me to appeal to diverse audiences while also engaging in the scientific version of full disclosure.

Some Final Words of Introduction

Having set the stage with a basic introductory description of my study, including the four issues just outlined, I now turn to my actual investigation of the learning of children from Mexican immigrant families at the start of their educational careers in the U.S. educational system. Let me be perfectly clear at the onset: This study is not working from some sort of "deficit" model that blames inequality on Mexican immigrant families themselves, nor is it working from a "revolutionary" model intended to pull the cloak off the systemic forces at work in creating this inequality. Instead, I work from the premise that the inequality facing children from Mexican immigrant families exists and is years in the making, and then I assess what will happen to this inequality if certain areas of their lives and their environments are targeted for help and assistance. Yes, the design of this study is complex, and so is the story it tells. At its core, however, is the simple aim of putting us in the business of ensuring that the dreams that bring people to the United States become something else entirely: reality.

Studying Children from Mexican Immigrant Families

INTERWOVEN AS IT IS WITH THE FABRIC OF AMERICAN SOCIETY, immigration has long been a major focal point of social and behavioral research in the United States. How immigration has been studied, however, has changed dramatically because the qualitative and quantitative nature of immigration has evolved over the last century.[1] A little backstory on immigration and immigration research is in order, therefore, before jumping to the specific topic of contemporary children from Mexican immigrant families.

The United States was built on immigration. That part of the American legend, at least, is true. Immigration—both voluntary and involuntary—has been the driving force of the U.S. population and the lifeblood of the U.S. economy for centuries. Throughout history, legal immigration has flowed into the United States primarily from Europe (obviously not counting the slave trade from Africa). This flow was supported by strict regional restrictions on immigration, such as the notorious Chinese exclusion laws in California in the late nineteenth and early twentieth centuries, that ensured that most immigrant families were White ethnics (e.g., Irish, Italian). This Eurocentric phenomenon was radically altered by changing economic circumstances in the mid-twentieth century and, ultimately, by new federal legislation in the 1960s that eliminated many of the systematic restrictions on immigration to the United States from Latin America and Asia. In the last four decades immigration has flowed primarily from these two regions, with Mexico representing the largest immigration stream, legal and illegal, of all.[2]

This rapidly increasing heterogeneity of the immigrant population in the United States has had far-reaching effects, not the least of which is an increasingly critical appraisal of popular and scientific conceptions of the immigrant experience. Specifically, a deeply ingrained notion in American culture is that immigrants can eventually attain social mobility through hard work, assimilation, and acculturation, but this notion does not hold true in the aggregate for modern immigrant families. Immigrants from different parts of the world come to the United States with different backgrounds, skills, statuses, and resources that put them on an uneven playing field in terms of their opportunities to succeed, the degree to which they are welcomed and accepted, their ability to blend in, and what they have to offer the host nation. Consequently, assimilation is a much rockier road for many in the modern era.[3] In many circles, therefore, new models of immigration have taken hold that collectively recognize that the heterogeneity of contemporary immigration has led to a corresponding heterogeneity of immigrant adaptation. On one hand, this heterogeneity is driven by diversity in *origins*. On the other hand, it is driven by diversity in *entry points*.

Consider first the origins of immigration to the United States, which are central to many of the social and economic models of immigrant adaptation. Some immigrants come from less developed regions of the world. They often have rural backgrounds and tend to be less well educated, have fewer job skills, and less proficiency in English. Importantly, these immigrants are often non-White, and they are more likely to have entered the United States through unauthorized, or illegal, means. Other immigrants come from more developed areas, or, alternatively, they come from less developed countries with long histories of sending well-educated, skilled workers to the United States. Such immigrants bring with them more resources, whether it be their training, education, language, or residency documents. Obviously, the prospects of the second group are much greater in the long run, not just in terms of socioeconomic success but also in terms of how well they will adapt to and be accepted by American culture. By achieving upward mobility much faster, they will conform to those traditional notions of the immigrant experience. The first group, however, will be hard-pressed to duplicate these upward trajectories, and, quite possibly, their origins may even contribute to downward trajectories over time and across generations.[4]

Now consider the entry points of immigration into the United States, which, of course, are closely related to origins. The segmented assimilation model is a good example of a perspective that prioritizes the sorting power of entry points. Different immigrant groups are absorbed into disparate segments of the class system and the racial/ethnic hierarchy of the United States. Those entering the more advantaged segments, by virtue of their origins but also by what they brought with them and how they look, will have access to better schools, safer neighborhoods, open job markets, and better connected social networks, all of which will promote higher, and faster, rates of upward mobility. Assimilation will be a positive and rewarding experience in this case. Those entering the more disadvantaged segments, however, will be served by more disorganized social institutions and will be frozen out of the kinds of information and assistance flows that provide advantages to the middle and upper classes in the job market. For these reasons their patterns of mobility will be stagnant over time and across generations.[5]

Bringing these themes together paints a somewhat distressing picture. Both origin point and entry point can be self-fulfilling phenomena, with advantages begetting advantages and disadvantages accumulating over time.

Children from Mexican Immigrant Families in the United States

So, where do the children of Mexican immigrants fit into this process? In general, Mexican-origin families capture the riskier side of the modern immigrant experience. First, the vast majority of Mexican immigrants are low-skilled labor migrants from rural areas who have low rates of educational attainment and English proficiency and high rates of poverty. These general characteristics are obstacles to securing steady, stable employment and to passing on valuable financial and social resources to the next generation. Second, many of these immigrants are undocumented, which makes finding work and accessing many societal institutions (e.g., health care, schools) difficult and which attaches a stigma to all Mexican immigrants regardless of their legal status. Third, Mexican immigrants are assigned to a lower ethnic status in a national culture in which skin color and language are key ingredients in social position. This lower status blocks the flow of services and resources to Mexican immigrant families, even those who are relatively more advantaged. For these reasons the road to social mobility—the American dream—is not an easy one for Mexican immigrants. Specifically, if assimilation entails the gradual movement away from cultural traditions of the old society toward those of the new society, then the assimilation of Mexican immigrants likely strips away many of the cultural resources brought from Mexico but *without* any commensurate infusion of new socioeconomic resources from the United States.[6]

As for the children of these families, this interplay of origin and entry points often means poor health care, bad schools, frequent stressors and upheavals, disorganized neighborhoods, discrimination, weak ties between home and school, and unsteady finances, all of which make educational attainment much harder, which, in turn, makes social mobility more challenging. These disadvantages also imperil, over time, the genuine noneconomic resources enjoyed by these children, such as the strong intergenerational networks that undergird their lives and protect them as well as the special strengths of their parents that allowed them to make the immigrant journey in the first place. If children are indeed the future, this twofold process, in which disadvantages eventually overwhelm advantages, implies that the future of the Mexican-origin population is at risk.[7] Generational declines, in which outcomes become more negative over time and across generations, will occur.

Indeed, a great deal of scientific evidence has documented this generational decline among Mexican-origin youth. Demographic analyses of nationally representative samples of adolescents, such as the National Educational Longitudinal Study (NELS) and the National Longitudinal Study of Adolescent Health (Add Health), have revealed that Mexican-origin adolescents tend to do worse than White adolescents in school but that, within the Mexican-origin population, recent immigrants do better than others.[8] Intensive high school–based ethnographies in California and Texas have replicated this pattern over the years.[9]

The explanation for these generational declines lies in the mixture of existing socioeconomic disadvantages and lost cultural resources that occur during the immigration and assimilation process. Three aspects of this issue should be highlighted. First, the apparent overperformance of immigrant adolescents within the Mexican-origin population does not necessarily mean that they are doing great. They are indeed at risk in U.S. schools compared to many of their classmates, just less so than other Mexican-origin youth. Second, despite this overall risk, this overperformance hints at a potential bright spot that often goes overlooked. That the most socioeconomically disadvantaged sector of the Mexican-origin population does the best suggests that Mexican immigrant adolescents may have a good chance at succeeding with a little more investment. Third, the heavy adolescent focus of this research has done a great deal to document inequalities related to Mexican immigration in the stage of formal schooling most immediate to labor force entry, but it has left uninvestigated the roots of these inequalities.

What we need to complement this growing body of evidence is renewed attention to the children who eventually grow up to be the subjects of adolescent-focused studies. What are the origins of the academic risks among children from Mexican immigrant families? How does their entry into formal schooling set the stage for the later patterns of academic achievement and educational attainment that have been so well documented? What are the specific investments that can be made to guard against this risk? Answering these questions is crucial to improving the long-term prospects of these children and to eliminating patterns of generational decline, because these children are the future parents of native-born Mexican-origin children.

The Early Childhood Longitudinal Study

Fortunately, the federal government has supported the collection of data that will help to answer these questions on a national scale. As mentioned in Chapter 1, data for the Early Child Longitudinal Study–Kindergarten Cohort (ECLS-K) were collected by the National Center for Education Statistics (NCES) of the U.S. Department of Education. Although a full description of the ECLS-K is included in the Appendix, here I provide an overview of what this data collection entailed.

In the late 1990s the NCES identified and recruited a large number of families from all across the United States.[10] Each of these families included one child who was to be enrolled in kindergarten in 1998. This sample was designed to be nationally representative of U.S. kindergartners, meaning that its demographic composition (e.g., race or ethnic group, geographic, socioeconomic breakdown) corresponded to the demographic composition of the entire U.S. population of kindergarten-age children. The final sample included 22,782 children attending kindergarten in more than 1,000 elementary schools in the fall of 1998. During the fall of 1998 (corresponding to the first half of kindergarten), each child took a series of diagnostic tests and their parents, teachers, and school principals were interviewed. This same protocol was followed in the second half of kindergarten (spring 1999), the second half of first grade (spring 2000), and the second half of third grade (spring 2002). Of course, the ECLS-K was not able to keep track of all 22,782 families. Some families dropped out of the study, others were lost. As a result, approximately 72 percent of the original children were still part of the ECLS-K four years after its inception. Although we would certainly like that to be 100 percent, this level of retention is quite good considering the great demands of large-scale, nationwide data collection.

The ECLS-K has a lot to recommend it to this particular study. First, as a large, nationally representative sample, it contains a sizable population of

Mexican-origin children, including those from immigrant families, that can be systematically compared to other racial or ethnic populations. Second, the ECLS-K targeted the start of formal schooling, first grade, with data from both before and after this transition. Third, the ECLS-K culled from numerous sources a broad array of information on several dimensions of children's lives. For example, parents reported on the health of their children as well as on their child care histories, teachers observed their students' in-school behaviors, school administrators described the elementary schools that the children attended, and children themselves completed diagnostic assessments in language use and other cognitive skills. This wealth of information provides a strong foundation for the multidimensional consideration of both the domains and contexts of child development. Fourth, at each stage of data collection, children took standardized tests in math and other core subjects. Not only do these tests gauge the level of learning at various stages of schooling, but they also allow the assessment of how learning evolves over time. Thus both the scope and the depth of the ECLS-K facilitate the investigation of a school transition model aimed directly at the burgeoning population of children from Mexican immigrant families.

For the purposes of this study I chose to examine a subset of the ECLS-K data. Specifically, I limited the original sample to the 13,003 children who met three specific criteria: (1) They were either White, African-American, Asian-American, or Latino/a; (2) they participated in the kindergarten, first-grade, and third-grade data collections; and (3) they had parents and teachers who were interviewed during the kindergarten data collection. Imposing these criteria did change the overall makeup of the sample. For the most part the original children in the ECLS-K sample who were not a part of this study tended to be more socioeconomically disadvantaged and more residentially mobile than those who were part of this study, and they were more likely to belong to a racial or ethnic minority group (see Table A1 in the Appendix for a detailed comparison). Yet these differences were in no way extreme, and the use of sampling weights (again, see the Appendix) helped to maintain the representative nature of the sample.

Defining Terms

In the ECLS-K parents reported the race or ethnicity of their children. With this information I was able to identify the proportion of my study sample accounted for by various races or ethnic groups. White children were the largest group (7,748 children), followed by 1,802 African-American children, 1,591 Latino/a children, and 1,093 Asian-American children. Parents also named the country in which their children, and they themselves, were born. These two pieces of information could be combined to identify all 769 children from Mexican immigrant families, a subset of the Latino/a population. These children were born in Mexico and immigrated to the United States at a young age, or they were born in the United States to Mexican-born parents who had earlier immigrated to the United States. I was also able to use this national origin information to identify White, African-American, Asian-American, and non-Mexican Latino/a children from immigrant families. Although non-Mexican immigrant distinctions are not central to the aims of this study, in the analyses reported in subsequent chapters of this book I did take into account that some of the non-Mexican children had immigrant backgrounds. Thus I refer to children in these comparison populations as "native" throughout the book.

As noted earlier, race or ethnic group and immigrant status overlap considerably with socioeconomic status in American society, and so any investigation of race or ethnicity must also take into account immigrant status. Fortunately, the ECLS-K also collected extensive socioeconomic information on its sample families. Parents reported on their own educational attainment, occupational attainment, and earnings. For the convenience of researchers using the ECLS-K, the NCES collapsed together all these different pieces of information to create a single scale measuring the socioeconomic status of each family. This scale ranges from −5 to 3, but the numbers on this scale have no intuitive meaning. Basically, higher scores imply higher socioeconomic status. Because a score of 0 represents the socioeconomic status of the average family in the ECLS-K, positive scores indicate families with above-average socioeconomic status and negative scores indicate families with below-average socioeconomic status.

This scale, however, was not the only piece of socioeconomic information of use in the ECLS-K. The earnings information that went into it could also be used to characterize families in another way. Dividing annual family income by the number of family members in the household gives the per capita income for the family. This number can then be compared to the federal poverty line, the criterion set by the federal government through a complex process to identify the "poor" in the United States. If a family's per capita income fell below the poverty line for their family size in 1998, then that family was designated as poor—2,320 families in the ECLS-K (approximately 18% of the sample). The families in the ECLS-K, as in the United States as a whole, demonstrated remarkable diversity in their basic compositional structures. The norm was for children to live with both of their biological parents who themselves were married (70%), with a roughly equal breakdown of the remainder living with one parent alone (usually a mother) or in a stepfamily (usually a mother and stepfather). In these different types of families some parents worked full-time, others did not. Their employment histories allowed me to identify how many parents fell into each category. Of those fathers who were present and provided employment information, most worked at least 35 hours per week (92%), with the remainder working either part-time or not at all. The majority of present mothers who reported employment information also worked (46% full-time, 23% part-time).

The original school transition model formulated by Alexander and Entwisle considers how race or ethnicity and socioeconomic status affect early learning. In this adaptation of the school transition model, learning is gauged by child performance on standardized tests in math. At each stage of data collection in the ECLS-K, children took short, timed tests in math. These tests included items on conceptual knowledge, procedural knowledge, problem solving, number sense, number properties and operations, and measurement. Scores on these tests were calculated according to item response theory (IRT) (see Appendix), a method that generates comparable scores across different kinds of tests taken at different stages. These IRT scores range from about 6 to 120 over the study years, with scores much lower and score ranges much narrower in the early years, as would be expected, given that the math instruction that occurs during formal schooling boosts performance on these tests over time. In the fall semester of kindergarten the average score on the math test was 22.08 in this sample. This average score rose to 55.47 by the spring semester of first grade, and then to 82.22 by the spring semester of third grade. In short, children's learning grew at a steady, and increasing, rate across the early years of elementary school.

A Rough Comparison of Children from Different Backgrounds

The 769 children from Mexican immigrant families were, of course, the focal point of this study, especially how they stack up with their peers in U.S. elementary schools. Table 2.1 gives a general picture of the breakdown of children from various racial, ethnic, and immigrant populations in the sample for this study (Table A2 in the Appendix designates statistically significant differences in these numbers).

Table 2.1 Breakdown of Five Racial/Ethnic and Immigrant Populations in the ECLS-K

Characteristic	Mexican Immigrant Family (%)	White (%)	African-American (%)	Other Latino/a (%)	Asian-American (%)
Demographic information					
Residence in South	27.1	31.4	60.9	27.7	13.8
Residence in Northeast	2.1	22.5	15.0	18.7	12.4
Residence in Midwest	6.9	32.5	16.0	14.0	17.7
Residence in West	64.0	13.6	8.1	39.6	56.1
Residence in large city	66.5	28.9	51.6	56.1	44.3
Residence in suburb	29.9	42.6	34.5	34.1	35.9
Residence in rural area	3.6	28.4	13.9	9.8	19.9
Socioeconomic information					
Family in poverty	49.0	7.9	38.7	26.0	20.2
Child lives with two married parents	78.7	77.3	33.1	62.2	78.9
Mother works full-time[a]	26.0	38.6	50.8	41.3	42.2
Mother works part-time	11.6	24.0	11.0	18.4	14.1
Mother not working	49.3	26.5	24.5	29.4	28.6
No mother present	0.6	1.3	1.4	1.6	1.6
Father works full-time[a]	65.0	74.7	33.5	58.8	66.8
Father works part-time	4.0	2.2	1.7	3.8	3.8
Father not working	4.8	2.7	4.3	5.2	6.0
No father present	11.1	10.6	48.2	22.4	9.9
Demographic information					
Average age (years)	6.2	6.3	6.2	6.2	6.1
Socioeconomic information					
Average family socioeconomic status (-5 to 3)	-0.7	0.3	-0.4	-0.2	0.2
Math achievement information					
Average fall kindergarten math score (6−98)	15.4	24.1	18.2	18.9	23.8
Average spring first-grade math score (8−108)	47.1	59.1	47.2	51.2	55.3
Average spring third-grade math score (3−121)	75.7	89.4	73.9	81.1	86.7
n	769	7,748	1,802	1,586	1,093

[a] For parental employment variables, a fifth category (missing employment information) is not shown.

To begin, children from Mexican immigrant families were concentrated in large urban areas in the West and were unlikely to live in northeastern and midwestern suburbs. They also were younger than their peers (except Asian-American children) upon entering kindergarten, which may pose a learning disadvantage.

More interesting, and more telling, are the racial/ethnic and immigration-related differences in the socioeconomic and academic factors. Mexican immigrant families had, by far, the lowest level of socioeconomic status and the highest rate of poverty in the sample. Nearly *one-half* of Mexican immigrant families reported an annual income *below* the federal poverty line. No other group even approached this poverty rate. These economic struggles occurred despite a high rate (in both absolute and relative terms) of two-parent families in this population, possibly because mothers in Mexican immigrant families were much less likely than other mothers to work outside the home. Although this low rate of maternal employment could have some positive effects on family life, it does constrain family earnings. Not surprisingly, given these socio-economic patterns, children from Mexican immigrant families had the lowest scores on the math achievement test in every year. The gap between them and their White peers grew by over 5 points from kindergarten to third grade.

These comparative statistics undergird this study in three key ways: They demonstrate (1) that children from Mexican immigrant families transition into elementary school with lower levels of math learning than their peers, (2) that this learning differential tends to widen over the course of the early years of elementary school, and (3) that these patterns are likely tied to the socioeconomic characteristics that go hand in hand with immigration from Mexico. In the remaining chapters of this book I bring together these patterns by identifying the domains of development and the contexts of development that either contribute to or narrow the differences in early math achievement as related to emigration from Mexico.

3

Looking at Three Domains of Child Development

THE COURSE OF A CHILD'S GENERAL GROWTH AND MATURATION FOLLOWS MUL-TIPLE "RAILS"—how the body takes shape, how the mind evolves, how skills and talents emerge and solidify—that mix, intertwine, feed off each other, and constrain each other over time. These rails are *domains* of development, or specific categories of maturation and adaptation that are qualitatively different yet part of the larger whole that is the child. Three such domains are health, psychosocial development, and cognitive development. How are each of these three domains related to emigration from Mexico? In this chapter I try to answer that question, and, later in this book, I attempt to trace the potential consequences for early learning of any such immigration-related differences.

Health of Children from Mexican Immigrant Families

How children do in school, including how much they learn, is a function of much more than intelligence and innate ability. Numerous factors shape the learning curve in elementary school, including the most basic elements of how children feel.[1] Thus understanding the roots of learning and of inequalities in learning requires a careful examination of how children feel, both in their bodies and in their minds. In this way health is a developmental domain that links Mexican immigrant status to early learning in school.

The first dimension of health considered here is physical, including what are referred to as global ratings of physical health that cover general states of malaise and poor health as well as inventories of acute physical health problems that catalog specific physiological complications with consequent symptoms and treatments. The second dimension of health considered here is mental, including both internalizing symptoms (e.g., suppressing emotional distress) and externalizing symptoms (e.g., acting out). The general premise is that when children feel bad either physically or mentally, they have more trouble doing well in school. Certainly, scientific evidence from a variety of sources supports this general premise.

First, general poor health as well as acute physical health problems, such as asthma or diabetes, has been shown to complicate academic progress in both elementary and secondary school, with progress measured by both earned grades in coursework and performance on standardized tests. The reasons for this linkage between physical health and academic performance certainly conform to common sense. Not only do physical health complications hamper brain development, but they also disrupt classroom attendance, concentration on in-class and out-of-class assignments, student-teacher bonding, and participation in school activities and the daily social life of schools. All these things take some level of effort, and mustering such effort becomes much more difficult when children are in pain or discomfort or when they require numerous trips to the doctor's office and/or adherence to medication schedules.[2] Indeed, one of the fundamental tenets of the classic Perry Preschool Project, an experiment in comprehensive early child care that has been tracked by social and behavioral scientists for decades, was that good health is absolutely crucial to early learning and achievement precisely because the absence of good health is such an enormous academic distraction.[3]

Second, both internalizing symptoms, such as signs of depression and anxiety, and externalizing symptoms, such as conduct disorder and aggression, have been linked empirically to lower grades and test scores in small school-based samples and in national data sets. This linkage between mental health and accepted markers of academic progress covers the full grade range of schooling, from the start of elementary school to the end of high school. Again, the mechanisms underlying this linkage are hardly surprising. Children who demonstrate internalizing and externalizing symptomatology have much greater difficulty staying on task in the classroom and getting all their work done. For these reasons they tend to fall behind. Unfortunately, they also suffer in other areas of schooling, which makes catching up even harder. For example, they are less likely to maintain positive goal orientations in the face of academic struggles, and they also experience far greater risk of social isolation in school because they have trouble connecting to other children in the classroom and forming strong relationships with their teachers.[4] In other words, because so much of schooling is social and emotional, success in school is endangered by mental health problems.

Thus both physical and mental health problems are risk factors for early learning difficulties. The extent to which children from Mexican immigrant families differ from their peers in physical and mental health before the start of elementary school, therefore, will translate into differences in learning once they enter elementary school classrooms.

Physical Health

So, where do children from Mexican immigrant families stack up in terms of physical health at the starting gate of the educational system? Some evidence suggests that they probably enter elementary school with more problematic physical health profiles than their native peers from other racial or ethnic populations, despite some potential counterevidence to this general trend that has generated a good deal of attention in scientific circles.

I begin with the counterevidence. Demographic surveys have consistently revealed the paradoxical findings that infants from Mexican immigrant families enjoy better birth outcomes than other U.S. infants, and other national-level research has frequently documented that adolescents from Mexican immigrant families have generally healthier lifestyles (e.g., avoidance of alcohol use, smoking, and other risky behaviors) than their peers.[5] Between these two poles, however, children from Mexican immigrant families do not fare as well. For example, demographic surveys, such as the Hispanic Health and Nutrition Examination Survey (HHANES) and the U.S. census, have detailed a trend in which Mexican-American youth, especially those born into immigrant families, rate themselves (and are rated by parents) as having poorer overall heath than the general U.S. population.[6] As for specific health complications, Mexican-origin children typically have higher than average rates of obesity, asthma, stunted growth, diabetes, and other problems, although these differentials typically fade, and even reverse, across the early life course.[7]

These same trends are also evident in the sample of young children examined in this study. In the ECLS-K, parents rated the general physical health of their children on a scale from 1 (poor health) to 5 (excellent health) during the fall semester of kindergarten. Such a global rating is one of the most commonly used and informative indicators of physical health in scientific research.[8] I reversed this rating, so that higher scores referred to poorer health, and then examined whether children from Mexican immigrant families scored higher on this scale than other children in the ECLS-K sample.

The *first* comparison of children from Mexican immigrant families to other children on the global rating of poor health (comparing all families) held constant sex, age, region of the country in which the children resided (Northeast, South, West, Midwest), and type of community in which the children resided (urban, suburban, rural). It also accounted for the fact that some of the White, African-American, Asian-American, and other Latino/a children had immigrant parents. It did not take family socioeconomic circumstances into account, which means that comparisons were made among all families regardless of whether they had the same or different socioeconomic circumstances.

The *second* comparison of children from Mexican immigrant families to other children on the global rating of poor health (comparing families with similar socioeconomic status), however, also held constant several important aspects of family socioeconomic background, including a comprehensive socioeconomic status ranking, family poverty, family structure, and parental employment (as well as some specific health-related factors, such as the physical health and depression of parents and the child's access to health care). In this comparison children were compared only to other children with similar family backgrounds. In other words, like was compared to like in terms of family socioeconomic circumstances. The difference between the two comparisons revealed the degree to which any observed immigration effects were channeled through family circumstances. This same comparison strategy and terminology will be used throughout this chapter and throughout the rest of the book.

Figure 3.1 is a graphical representation of both comparisons. Specifically, it contains the predicted level of poor physical health for the average child in each population of interest, calculated from the results of each comparison (see Table A3 in the Appendix for full results of these comparisons). As seen in the first comparison of Figure 3.1 (comparing all families), Mexican immigrant parents reported that their children had poorer physical health, in global terms, than did native White, African-American, Asian-American, and other Latino/a parents.

According to the second comparison in Figure 3.1 (comparing families with similar socioeconomic status), taking family socioeconomic characteristics into account substantially reduced the distance between children from

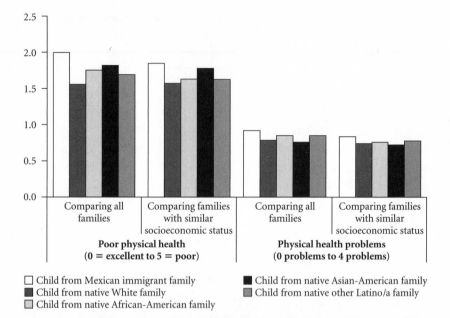

Figure 3.1 Predicted level of physical health of average child in five populations

Mexican immigrant families and their native peers on poor physical health but, with one exception, did not make this distance disappear completely. Children from Mexican immigrant families had poorer physical health than White, African-American, and other Latino/a children with similar family socioeconomic profiles. Once family socioeconomic characteristics were taken into account, Mexican immigrant and Asian-American parents reported that their children had roughly similar levels of physical health.

Ideally, cataloging physical health complications would cover a broad spectrum of health disorders and conditions, including asthma, diabetes, and obesity. Unfortunately, the ECLS-K asked parents about only a small number of such complications. Specifically, during the fall semester of kindergarten, parents reported whether or not their children had suffered from repeated ear infections, vision problems, and hearing problems in the past year. Measurements of the height and weight of all children allowed the calculation of body mass index (BMI). BMI is the ratio of weight to height that is used by the Centers for Disease Control and Prevention to identify overweight children (those who have a BMI at or above the 85th percentile for their age and sex). For each child in the ECLS-K, I counted how many of these four physical health complications they had experienced and then compared children from Mexican immigrant families to native children on this factor in the same way, as described earlier.

As seen in the predicted number of physical health complications presented in the third comparison of Figure 3.1 (comparing all families), children from Mexican immigrant families generally experienced more complications than their White and Asian-American peers. These differences were reduced, but not eliminated, when family socioeconomic factors were taken into account (see the last comparison of families with similar socioeconomic status in Figure 3.1), indicating that some of the apparent health disadvantage of these children was, in part, a function of their lower socioeconomic status. Children from Mexican immigrant families also experienced more physical health complications than their African-American and other Latino/a peers, although these differences were somewhat smaller. Interestingly, these same differences increased when family socioeconomic factors were held constant, indicating that the lower family socioeconomic characteristics of children from Mexican immigrant families actually masked even greater health differentials compared to African-American and other Latino/a children. In other words, children from Mexican immigrant families would look even worse health-wise if not given "credit" (for lack of a better term) for their more disadvantaged backgrounds.

Mental Health

When assessing the relative health of children from Mexican immigrant families at the transition to elementary school, I also wanted to consider mental health. Much less research has examined the mental health outcomes of Mexican immigrant children than has examined their physical health, but evidence from related scientific studies is telling and helped to guide my expectations for this investigation. First, demographic analyses of nationally representative data on immigrant adolescents, not just those from Mexico, have revealed that immigrants tend to have better psychological outcomes (e.g., positive outlook) than their native-born peers, regardless of national origin and race or ethnicity. Some, but not all, of these advantages are due to social class differences.[9] Second, school-based ethnographies that focused specifically on the Mexican-American population in California and Texas, the two largest receiving states of Mexican immigrants to the United States, have repeatedly demonstrated that Mexican immigrant youth have high levels of psychological adjustment and low levels of conduct disorder. These young people tend to feel more secure, largely because of the intergenerational ties to their families and communities that undergird their lives.[10]

These related studies, therefore, point to a potential mental health pattern for children from Mexican immigrant families that is diametrically opposed to the corresponding physical health pattern laid out earlier. In short, this evidence suggests that children from Mexican immigrant families will have better mental health than their peers from native racial or ethnic populations. In other words, they might have an advantage in mental health that balances out their disadvantage in physical health.

To examine this possibility, I looked at two markers of mental health from the ECLS-K. During the fall semester of kindergarten, teachers reported on the extent to which they had observed signs of internalizing symptoms (e.g., anxiety, sadness) in the child at school as well as the extent to which they had observed signs of externalizing symptoms (e.g., anger, fighting). Scientists who study the health and well-being of children broadly accept both types of symptoms as markers of mental health problems.[11]

In studies of older children and adolescents, researchers can ask the young people themselves about their feelings and behaviors, but that is not appropriate in studies of young children, who have a less developed sense of self, less ability to be introspective, and fewer language skills to articulate their feelings. For these reasons studies of children typically rely on expert evaluations or reports by "neutral" observers. This last type of child-specific method is the most efficient and cost-effective for large-scale, national-level data collections, hence the use of teacher observations in the ECLS-K. Although conventionally accepted, these teacher reports are not perfect. After all, teachers are human too and, as such, may be colored by the same cultural stereotypes as any other person. Moreover, teachers certainly do not spend all day with their students and, consequently, may not have access to full information about the children's thoughts and actions. Thus teacher reports may be somewhat biased, especially when students and teachers come from different backgrounds, but these biases are countered by the many advantages that these reports offer.

With these caveats in mind, I compared children from Mexican immigrant families to their native peers from other racial and ethnic populations on these two markers of mental health problems. Again, the first comparison involved all families (controlling for sex, age, region of the country, type of community), and the second comparison involved families with similar socioeconomic cir-

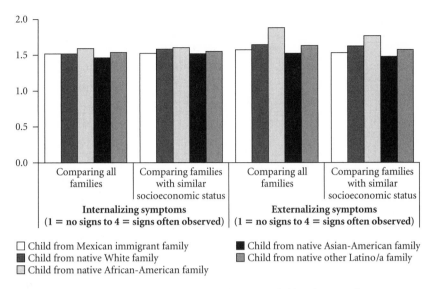

Figure 3.2 Predicted level of mental health of average child in five populations

cumstances (also controlling for parents' health and their children's access to health care). The full results of these comparisons are contained in Table A4 in the Appendix. The predicted levels of internalizing and externalizing symptoms calculated from these comparisons are presented in Figure 3.2.

As seen in the first comparison of Figure 3.2, comparing all families revealed that children from Mexican immigrant families had lower levels of internalizing symptoms than their African-American peers but roughly equal levels to their White, Asian-American, and other Latino/a peers. As seen in the second comparison of Figure 3.2, taking family socioeconomic characteristics into account altered this basic pattern in one crucial way. When comparing children of similar family backgrounds, children from Mexican immigrant families had slightly but significantly lower levels of internalizing symptoms than both their African-American and White peers. Turning to the third comparison in Figure 3.2, the average child from a Mexican immigrant family had a lower predicted level of externalizing symptoms than his or her White, African-American, and other Latino/a counterparts. Holding family socioeconomic characteristics equal across populations (final comparison in Figure 3.2) reduced but did not eliminate the differences compared to the average White and African-American child but did eliminate completely the difference compared to the average other Latino/a child.

Health Summary

Based on these results, health is a developmental domain that likely plays some role in population-level differences in early learning related to Mexican immigration. Children from Mexican immigrant families generally had fairly good health in absolute terms, but in relative terms they fared worse *and* better than their native peers. This pattern echoes the findings of research that I conducted earlier on immigrant children in general.[12]

Beginning with the negative side of things, children from Mexican immigrant families tended to be less physically healthy than most of their peers from other racial or ethnic populations at the start of kindergarten. If physical health is indeed related to early learning in first grade and beyond, then this physical health disadvantage is an academic risk factor. Turning to the positive side, these children tended to be mentally healthier than some of their peers and no less mentally healthy than their other peers at the start of kindergarten. If mental health is related to subsequent learning trajectories, then this mental health advantage could be an academic resource.

These results suggest, therefore, that physical health disadvantages and mental health advantages of children from Mexican immigrant families when they enter elementary school may cancel each other out as elementary school progresses. If so, then studying only one dimension of health could be quite misleading when considering educational experiences in this large and growing population. Either one alone gives an incomplete picture, one too rosy and one too bleak.

Psychosocial Development of Children from Mexican Immigrant Families

When children transition into elementary school, they are making a huge leap from the private world of their families to the public world of formal societal organizations that will dominate the rest of their lives. For the first time in what will prove to be a long line of doing so, they must learn how to function in a formal setting in which they have to work with others, follow rules, perform tasks, and face external evaluations that determine rewards and advancement. In this way elementary school can be thought of as an early point on the broad spectrum that is work life in the United States.[13] Just as in work in other stages of the life course, performance in this setting, as well as the assessment of performance in this setting, is a function of how well individuals can get along with others and how well they can control their own behaviors and actions. Thus where children are in terms of their psychological and social development when they enter elementary school goes a long way toward shaping how they do academically during these years of schooling.[14] As such, psychosocial development is an important domain to consider when assessing learning differences between children from Mexican immigrant families and their peers in the early years of elementary school even if, on face value, it does not appear to fall within the sphere of schooling.

Let's begin with a psychological dimension of psychosocial development. Self-regulation refers to the degree to which children can control their own behavior according to the expectations and demands of any given setting. Self-regulation is often thought of in terms of a collection of work-related skills that tap independence, self-control, and responsibility. Self-regulating children are able to follow the written and unwritten rules in the classroom or some other setting without being repeatedly instructed by adults—they know what they are supposed to do and they do it on their own or, at least, without extra encouragement.[15]

Although in many ways excessive conformity and obedience is antithetical to intellectual development, classrooms do run more smoothly when children are better behaved. After all, teachers can teach better when they are not distracted by other responsibilities in the classroom, such as continually commanding students to do this and do that. Moreover, students who are self-regulating are better able to engage in the school experience. They are, in a sense, ready to go when class starts and on task as class progresses, which allows them to spend maximum time on learning and to follow their learning activities through to completion.[16] Thus self-regulation is an important factor in early achievement.

As for the social dimension of psychosocial development, social competence refers to the degree to which children can interact with, form relationships with, and establish partnerships with their peers and, importantly, the extent to which they can avoid conflict in peer interactions, both one on one and in groups. Social competence encompasses the social skills that complement the work-related skills that fall under self-regulation.[17]

Obviously, such competence is an important element of life and a key ingredient of personal happiness. Yet the value of social competence goes beyond merely the subjective enjoyment of life; it also extends to the school domain and contributes to learning. How is that? Socially competent children are better able to forge strong ties with their teachers, which facilitates the passage of information, skills, and knowledge from old to young.[18] These children are also better able to work with other children in the classroom on both classroom projects and other nonassigned activities. Such cooperative experiences can become an added form of learning. Finally, children who have social competence become more integrated into the social activities of their schools, things such as play groups or games or even close friendships, and the feelings of happiness, security, and comfort fostered by this social integration really do open them up to learning.[19]

Thus elementary school is a new environment for children, and they must bring certain skills with them to this environment to succeed. Although not as obvious examples of skills as reading ability, self-regulation and social competence are indeed skills—in fact, important skills. To the extent that children from Mexican immigrant families differ from their peers on this strand of development, therefore, they will likely follow different learning curves in the first few years of schooling.

Self-Regulation

Although a good deal of scientific research has focused on immigrant youth in the United States, including those with Mexican roots, only a tiny portion of this attention has been paid to aspects of psychosocial development in young children. Consequently, I had to turn to related fields of study to be able to construct predictions about how children from Mexican immigrant families would compare to their peers from other racial or ethnic populations on the two aspects of psychosocial development mentioned here. In a sense, I was able to make an educated guess about what would happen based on similar but not identical comparisons.

Several insightful ethnographies of Mexican-origin high school students have been conducted in specific communities in Texas and California,[20] and one theme that has arisen from these ethnographies echoes larger scale research on immigrant youth, not just youth of Mexican origins, conducted in several states.[21] Specifically, teachers and other adults often have quite positive opinions about the behavior of immigrant youth in general and of Mexican immigrant youth in particular. They think that they are incredibly well behaved—obedient, respectful, conscientious, and compliant. These opinions suggest that Mexican-origin youth are better able to control themselves and their behavior in the classroom than their peers, which, in turn, suggests that they are more self-regulating. In other words, they know how to act when they are at school.

This same pattern likely extends to the specific case of children from Mexican immigrant families.

During the fall semester of kindergarten, teachers were asked to rate the ECLS-K children in their classrooms according to six dimensions of work orientation. For example, they reported how often—on a 4-point scale, where 1 = never and 4 = often—they witnessed children demonstrating attentiveness, task persistence (e.g., completing their assignments), concentration, and organization. These reports were used to create a scale that the NCES labeled approaches to learning—the high average score on this scale in the ECLS-K sample (3.02 out of 4) indicates that teachers were generally happy with how their students tackled the business of school. This approaches-to-learning scale is the marker of self-regulation in my comparison of children from Mexican immigrant families to their native peers from other populations during kindergarten.

The first comparison in Figure 3.3 contains the predicted levels of self-regulation that arose from my comparison of children from Mexican immigrant families and their native peers from other racial or ethnic populations

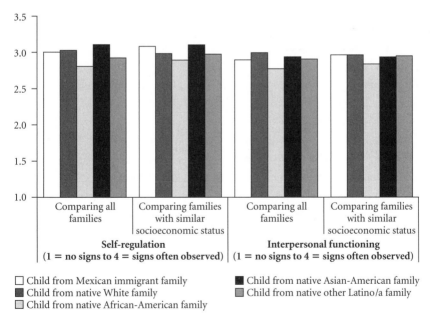

Figure 3.3 Predicted level of psychosocial development of average child in five populations

(see Table A5 in the Appendix for the full results of all comparisons on self-regulation). Elementary school teachers did not rate the children from Mexican immigrant families in their classrooms as being more self-regulated than their White peers, but they did think that they were more self-regulated than their African-American and other Latino/a peers. On the other hand, these teachers thought that their Asian-American students were the most self-regulated children in their classrooms, even more than children from Mexican immigrant or White families.

According to the second comparison in Figure 3.3, this general pattern changed when children from Mexican immigrant families were compared to peers with similar socioeconomic backgrounds. Now, children from Mexican immigrant families were rated by their teachers as being equally self-regulated as their Asian-American peers, and both of these populations were rated higher than their White, African-American, and other Latino/a peers.

Social Competence

Looking to past research on immigrant youth, including those of Mexican origins, to make predictions about how children from Mexican immigrant families stack up in terms of social competence is a little tricky because this past body of work seems to provide contradictory clues. On one hand, the clear pattern from qualitative and quantitative research (including my own ECLS-K work) is that immigrant youth are better behaved and more controlled in school than their peers, and one might suspect that this pattern would emerge on the playground too. In other words, these children's greater ability to regulate their own behavior would likely allow them to function better in play groups and in other interpersonal settings. On the other hand, one of the most striking themes of adolescent-focused research on immigration is that immigrant youth are much less peer oriented than the other students in their schools. They are focused more on their families and other adults than on their fellow students, are less involved in peer activities, and inhabit more peripheral positions in the peer networks of their schools. This is not surprising, of course, because these young people are trying to grapple with a new culture in a new country and may have trouble fitting in or even wanting to fit in at all.[22]

Thus past research in the area of social competence sends some mixed signals about what to expect, and so the children in the ECLS-K are left to settle the debate. To compare the social competence of children from Mexican immigrant families to that of their native peers from other racial or ethnic populations during kindergarten, I again turned to the extensive teacher reports provided by the ECLS-K. During the fall semester of kindergarten, teachers assessed the basic interpersonal skills of the children in their classrooms, including those children from Mexican immigrant families, as part of the extensive battery of assessments they made about various aspects of children's functioning in school (e.g., approaches to learning, internalizing and externalizing symptoms). Specifically, teachers rated children on a scale of 1 to 4 (again, low to high) on multiple aspects of social skills, sociability, and social relationships, including their ability to get along with others who were different, comforting or helping others, expressing feelings, ideas, and opinions in positive ways, and showing sensitivity to the feelings of others. On average, children scored fairly high on this scale (3.00 on a 4-point scale).

The remaining two comparisons in Figure 3.3 present the predicted levels of social competence for each population (see Table A5 in the Appendix for the full results that produced these predicted levels). When family socioeconomic circumstances were not taken into account (third comparison in Figure 3.3), African-American children were rated as being the least socially competent, White children the most, and children from Mexican immigrant families somewhere in the middle. When family socioeconomic circumstances were factored in (final comparison in Figure 3.3), children from Mexican immigrant families were roughly equivalent to most of their peers on social competence. In fact, all non-African-American children of the same family socioeconomic profile were fairly similar on the way their teachers rated their social competence, but African-American children were always rated lower.

Psychosocial Summary

As we saw with health earlier in this chapter, my investigation of psychosocial development revealed a mixed bag for children from Mexican immigrant families. They appeared to be more self-regulating than most of their peers and, moreover, were at least not substantially lower on social competence than most of their peers. Yet their family situations played a significant role in these comparisons.

Children from more disadvantaged family backgrounds ranked lower on the two aspects of psychosocial development (see Table A5 in the Appendix), and, of course, Mexican immigrant families were, on average, disadvantaged. Thus the average child from a Mexican immigrant family will not be as self-regulating or as highly functioning in interpersonal settings. The reasons for this pattern have more to do with their family resources than with their immigrant status, but that is certainly not an easy thing to tease apart in the everyday life of the elementary school.

Certain Cognitive Skills Among Children from Mexican Immigrant Families

One of the underlying, guiding themes of this book is that doing well (or poorly) in school, whatever the stage, is a product of many more things than innate ability or cognitive skills, that it is intricately and practically inextricably wrapped up with all the other "stuff" that goes on in students' lives that has nothing to do with the three R's. This theme, however, in no way implies that the more academic or cognitive aspects of students' growth and development play no role in their schooling careers. Obviously, these things matter a great deal. At their core, academic experiences are driven by a variety of intellectual competencies, and even those perspectives on education that are most acutely interested in the *social* aspects of schooling have to take these *individual* characteristics into account. In the many studies of elementary and secondary education that I have conducted over the years, I have seen no exception to this rule, and this particular book on children from Mexican immigrant families is no exception. Part of the reason that children from Mexican immigrant families are at risk in the early years of schooling is because of the transition into U.S. schools with different kinds of intellectual competencies.

Please, please note that I said *different*, not worse or inferior. By virtue of their bicultural, bilingual existence in the early stages of development, children from Mexican immigrant families obviously have important skills—skills most U.S. students can never match—that give them some edge in the classroom. At the same time, because of many of the same socioeconomic, linguistic, and community influences, children from Mexican immigrant families are also less developed in specific cognitive areas that might hinder their progress relative to other students. As detailed so eloquently by Angela Valenzuela in her book *Subtractive Schooling*, this difference *becomes* disadvantage when U.S. schools value the latter skills over the former, benefiting more Americanized patterns of socialization at the expense of other cultural traditions.

So, what are the skills that play into this problem? Two important areas come to mind: English-language proficiency and early math knowledge. Neither of these skills is innate. They do not simply exist in the child but instead are cultivated over time in an interplay of children's more innate competencies and their environments. Regardless of their origins, however, both skills matter a great deal in the U.S. educational system.

Think about language proficiency—children have to understand what their teachers are saying in order to be taught, they have to read what is given to them in order to learn. This is especially true in a curriculum such as math, in which the language of the subject is highly technical and somewhat divorced from everyday language comprehension.[23] Given the sorry state of bilingual instruction in the United States and the extremely low likelihood that texts will be translated into foreign languages (including Spanish), trouble understanding teachers or reading class materials will be a major obstacle to success in school in general and in the math curriculum in particular. Thus children who are not proficient in English will be more likely to fall behind in their studies, even when they might have excelled if taught in their native language.

Now, consider early math skills. In theory, teaching or instruction in math and exposure to math begins with the advent of elementary school, so that all children start off their schooling careers on an even playing field ready to be taught and to learn. In practice, of course, children enter school with wildly different levels of knowledge about and familiarity with mathematical concepts because of different interests, different home learning strategies, different parent abilities, different media exposure, and many other factors.[24] For example, one child may not be able to recognize numbers at all, a second may know how to count, a third may be able to do simple calculations by hand, and a fourth might be whipping up Excel spreadsheets. Which of these children will be in the best position to achieve in the early math curriculum, which has the best foundation on which to build a math career, which will be channeled into higher level ability groups, which will inspire the highest expectations among teachers? The answer is simple: Children who enter elementary school with more math knowledge will probably do better in math during elementary school, partly because they are given more opportunities to learn even if their actual aptitude in math is no different from their peers'. On the other hand, other children who are essentially introduced to math at the start of elementary school have much more ground to cover and are at risk for being tracked away from rewarding math curricula, even if they have high aptitude in math. Learning begets learning in a cycle of cumulative advantage.

Thus the U.S. educational system prioritizes certain cognitive skills and abilities over others. If these prioritized skills, such as English proficiency and early math knowledge, are less likely to be found among children from Mexican immigrant families, then these children will be less ably served by the system regardless of their actual intelligence or potential. The results of these different priorities are likely truncated learning trajectories in elementary school as children from Mexican immigrant families play a game of catch-up that their peers do not.

English-Language Proficiency

Some might argue that comparing rates of English-language proficiency in Mexican immigrant and other populations is something of a pointless task. *Of course*, children who are born in Mexico or who are being raised by parents who were born in Mexico are more likely to be less proficient in English than White children. After all, the overwhelming majority of White children are American-born and have American-born parents, and a good chunk of the remainder emigrated from English-speaking countries. This is hardly a fair competition. But what will emerge when children from Mexican immigrant families are compared to other racial or ethnic populations with stronger, more recent roots in other countries, such as Asian-American or other Latino/a children? Some evidence suggests that children from Mexican immigrant families will also lag behind these children in English proficiency because of socioeconomic disadvantages (e.g., low rates of parent education, poverty) but also because of their segregation into linguistically isolated communities and schools and because of low rates of preschool education.[25] If so, then children from Mexican immigrant families are at risk in their early educational careers relative to both native-born and immigrant peers.

Fortunately, identifying less English proficient children in the ECLS-K is possible. As I have already mentioned, a big part of the ECLS-K was the administration of achievement tests to all the sample children in math, reading, and general knowledge during each school year. Because English-language difficulties would obviously be a major obstacle to doing well on these tests, the NCES decided to first identify all low-English-proficient children. The NCES devised a comprehensive language test—the Oral Language Development Scale (OLDS)—and administered this test to all children whose parents reported speaking a non-English language at home. Children who fell below a specified threshold on this test were then deemed low English proficient. I then analyzed who was most likely to test in this low-proficiency range.

The full results of this analysis, for those who want to see them, are contained in Table A6 in the Appendix, but I can give the gist of the results here.

Children from all native non-White populations were more likely to have English-language problems than White children. For example, the average native child from a non-Mexican Latino/a family had odds of being low English proficient that were more than 20,000 times that of a native White child of the same sex, age, region, and urbanicity. As big as this difference is, it was dwarfed by the corresponding difference between native White children and children from Mexican immigrant families. Indeed, the difference in this comparison is of the order of 300,000 times. These children from Mexican immigrant families also had far, far greater odds of being low English proficient than their native Asian-American and African-American peers. Not surprisingly, all these differences decreased when children from similar socioeconomic backgrounds were compared, but they remained extraordinarily high nonetheless. These results leave no doubt that children from Mexican immigrant families enter U.S. schools, in which instruction (including the best instruction) is conducted in English, at a disadvantage relative to *all* their native peers.

Preschool Math Skills

Beyond language skills, how do children from Mexican immigrant families compare to their peers in early math skills—in other words, the math skills that they have cultivated before the start of formal instruction? Unfortunately, we know far less about school readiness in math than we do about school readiness in reading, and thus we know little about differences in entry-level math knowledge related to Mexican immigration other than what can be surmised from race and ethnic group comparisons in early math achievement.[26] What can be surmised is that children from Mexican immigrant families do indeed start school with less familiarity with math than many of their peers.

To actually test this educated guess, I examined racial/ethnic and immigration-related differences in math test scores at the beginning of kindergarten, which is the earliest starting point of instruction in the *formal* U.S. educational system. When the ECLS-K children took the timed math tests in the first months of kindergarten and answered questions about number sense and recognition, they were essentially being assessed on what math knowledge they had accrued, through various means, *before* entering school, what they brought with them into the classroom. In this way, their scores on these early tests represented their math "baseline" on which formal instruction will build over the years.

Table 3.1 contains the predicted scores on the initial math achievement test

Table 3.1 Predicted Math Test Scores in the Fall Semester of Kindergarten of the Average Child in the Five Study Populations

Population	Predicted Math Test Score (6 is minimum, 98 is maximum)	
	Comparing All Families	Comparing Families with Similar Socioeconomic Status
Child from Mexican immigrant family	16.86	18.51
Child from native White family	23.13	22.62
Child from native African-American family	18.98	20.19
Child from native Asian-American family	23.55	23.13
Child from native Latino/a family	19.04	20.04

in kindergarten in all five racial/ethnic populations, generated from the more complicated comparisons detailed and presented in Table A6 in the Appendix. Across populations, children scored low on this test, but children in some populations scored lower than others. Specifically, children from Mexican immigrant families scored, on average, significantly lower on the first kindergarten math test in the ECLS-K than all native children, but especially White and Asian-American children. As seen in the language proficiency results presented earlier in this chapter, this low relative standing was only partly accounted for by the more disadvantaged socioeconomic circumstances of Mexican immigrant families. In short, children from Mexican immigrant families tended to be less familiar with math when they started school than their peers.

Cognitive Summary

Cognitive development is certainly a broad topic, encompassing many different skills and competencies accrued and developed in many different ways. In two cognitive areas that are prioritized by U.S. schools, however, children from Mexican immigrant families tended to be somewhat behind their peers. Specifically, they were more likely to have trouble with English, and they were less familiar with math. Regardless of the other cognitive skills and advantages that they did bring with them to school and regardless of their actual intelligence, these two characteristics placed children from Mexican immigrant families at a disadvantage just when their actual educational careers were beginning.

Even more worrisome is the potential for U.S. educators, on the basis of their early evaluations of these entry-level skills, to shape the instruction and placement of children in self-fulfilling ways. For example, a teacher views a gifted Mexican immigrant child to be unintelligent because of her difficulty speaking English and, consequently, recommends that this child be placed in remedial coursework that provides no intellectual stimulation or challenge for that child and eventually causes her to disengage from school and do poorly. In this way the low level of English proficiency and early math skills characteristic of children from Mexican immigrant families could even trump their actual aptitudes and abilities.

4 Exploring Three Contexts of Child Development

IN THIS CHAPTER OUR FOCUS SHIFTS from domains of child development to contexts of child development. If domains refer to the different kinds of development, contexts refer to the settings in which these different kinds of development take place. To elaborate a little more, children live and grow within what is known as an ecology or an environment that consists of a set of interlocking, overlapping social settings. In these settings children are exposed to different kinds of people, roles, rules, materials, and resources, all of which come together in unique ways to shape how children turn out in the long run. Three of the key contexts of early childhood are families, child care, and schools, each of which is discussed in this chapter and each of which is eventually linked to immigration-related differences in early learning.

Home Environment of Mexican Immigrant Families

Ask anyone—a kid on the playground, a person on the street, a developmental psychologist, a politician—what the most important force is in young children's lives, and the answer will likely be the same: the family, or, to be more precise, parents. In American society parents bear the responsibility for raising children, although they certainly do not do it alone. That is why social and behavioral scientists refer to the family as the primary context of child development.[1] In this capacity the family is not simply a place where children are socialized into the ways of the world; the family also helps to select the other settings that will socialize children. In other words, what goes on in the family molds the child, but on top of that the family determines who and what else will mold the child and how.

This indirect and direct socializing role of the family is vividly captured in the transition to elementary school. Before formal schooling starts, parents are a powerful force in their children's development, and the things that they teach their children, the values that they instill in their children, the talents that they cultivate in their children, and the traits and qualities that they nurture in their children in these years influences the types of schools that their children will enter and, importantly, how their children will adapt to and function in these schools. In this way the most important developmental context of childhood, the family, lays the groundwork for the most important *extrafamilial* developmental context of childhood, the school. This is what is meant by the term home-school partnership. The parents at home and the teachers and personnel at school are in partnership during this critical period, even if they do not know it.[2]

How might this partnership between the home and the school be useful for understanding the early education of children from Mexican immigrant families? Certainly, the family is central to Mexican-American life. Much has been written and said about the concept of familism, which refers to the incredibly strong emphasis placed on family life and family connections in Mexican culture. The strength of Mexican immigrant families, therefore, is not the issue. If anything, the strong family bonds that have been found in Mexican immigrant families are a bonus for children from these families as they enter U.S. schools because they more than satisfy one of the most important tasks that families have in preparing children for educational success.[3] This resource is quite simple really, one that seems self-evident. It is providing a secure, stable foundation of love and emotional support for children so that they have the confidence to try new things, take chances, dare to fail, and really give their all to what they are doing.[4]

Other family processes, however, add to the benefits of emotional attachments and security in promoting school success, especially among young children just starting out on their way, and these processes may not be as common among Mexican immigrant families. They are more active in nature and tap the direct ways that parents prepare their children for school. For two reasons I concentrate on these processes in this book. First, because they are education focused, these processes are more likely to tap parents' conscious efforts to get their children school ready and, beyond that, to ensure that their children advance in school at a satisfactory rate. Second, these parenting strategies are more actionable in the sense that they can be taught in ways that emotional attachments cannot. Consequently, they are more likely to be targeted, and targeted successfully, by interventions and programs than the more intimate inner workings of parent-child relationships.[5]

To be more specific, the family processes that I am talking about are home learning activities, such as doing projects or artwork together, home reading activities, such as going through storybooks together, and parental involvement at school, such as meeting teachers and volunteering. *All* these parenting behaviors are connected to educational success. This connection does *not* arise merely because the parents who engage in these behaviors are better educated and wealthier—they typically are, but these behaviors are also educationally significant even when they are not. Together these activities cultivate important academic skills in children that they will need when they start school, build on what is learned in school, instill in children the motivation for learning and the desire to learn, demonstrate to children that their parents believe that schooling is important, allow parents to be more effective advocates for their children at school, and give parents better insight into how schools work.[6] Importantly, my past work in this area has shown that parents' active management of their children's education declines rapidly with age because educational trajectories become more rigidly set.[7] This finding implies that these behaviors will have the *most* impact at the start of elementary school.

The parenting behaviors that I have just described are probably the most common foci of researchers' attempts to understand the link between the family and the school, especially when looking at young children. I am going to throw another aspect of the home environment into the mix here, one that may not be so important in general child populations but is of the utmost importance in the Mexican immigrant population. That aspect is home language use, specifically whether and how often parents speak non-English languages to children attending U.S. schools. The language issue is often an emotional one, with widespread misconceptions about what bilingualism is, sharp disagreements about the value of bilingual education, debate over the ways in which language use facilitates the loss of culture, and somewhat distressing statistics about the connection between language use and education. This issue is especially controversial in states such as California that are the primary destination points of Mexican immigration.[8] What is clear is that, because U.S. schools are usually run in the English language and because they rarely cut much slack to non-English speakers, children who come from what is often referred to as linguistically isolated families face additional barriers in their educational careers because their non-English-speaking parents cannot participate in their English-language schooling to the same degree that other parents can. Emotional support is there, but practical and instrumental support is more difficult.[9] Although not explicitly education focused, home language use shares the commonality with other family processes considered in this chapter that it is something we can work with in the long term.

In the final analysis families can support their children's transition into elementary school in many ways. Of these many different strategies I focus on the ones that balance two needs: effecting academic improvements and being amenable to intervention. Home language use, learning activities, and reading activities strike such a balance, as does parental involvement at school. Given their likely importance in the transition to elementary school and their potential value as intervention points, uncovering any potential racial/ethnic and immigration-related variability in these parenting behaviors is of the utmost importance.

Home Language Use

In Chapter 3 I described the body of research reporting that Mexican immigrant youth in the United States are slower to learn English than their peers in other immigrant populations and pointing to the linguistic isolation of Mexican immigrant communities as a major factor in this phenomenon. The truth is that this isolation does not affect just the children of Mexican immigrant families; it also affects their parents.[10] Indeed, because children from Mexican immigrant families attend U.S. schools, they tend to be less linguistically isolated than their parents to the point that they often end up being family translators.[11] Again, this phenomenon covers the full range of the immigrant experience and is a fact of life in most ethnic enclaves in the United States, but it is especially pronounced in Mexican immigrant communities, which are larger and more numerous than others.

My analysis of the ECLS-K certainly supports this past research. When their children were in kindergarten, parents were asked what the dominant language of their family was and how often they used this language to speak to their children. Parents who said that they used a non-English language "very often" when speaking to their children got the highest score on my scale of non-English home language use, which ran from 1 to 4. As in past chapters, I then compared the five racial and ethnic populations in this study on home language use, first holding constant certain demographic characteristics

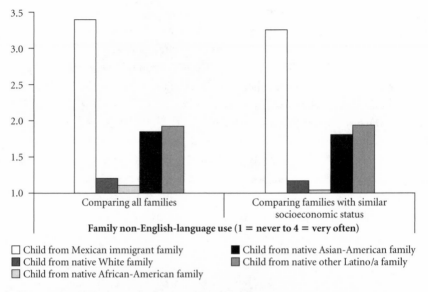

Figure 4.1 Predicted level of non-English-language use at home of average child in five populations

(e.g., sex) and then holding constant certain socioeconomic characteristics (e.g., family poverty). Table A7 in the Appendix contains the full results of these comparisons, and Figure 4.1 presents the results of these comparisons in a more accessible way.

Echoing what I reported on child language proficiency in Chapter 3, the first comparison in Figure 4.1 reveals that Mexican immigrant families were the most likely to use a non-English language (in this case, Spanish) when speaking to their children at home of all the racial and ethnic populations considered, not just compared to the native populations that are not currently being fueled by immigration (e.g., Whites, African-Americans) but also compared to native populations with a significant immigration history (e.g., Asian-Americans, other Latino/as). In fact, the average non-English usage in the Mexican immigrant population fell between "often" and "very often," but the average in the native populations, including Asian-American and other Latino/a families, fell below the "sometimes" level. This high rate of non-English language use at home—or, alternatively, low rate of English use at home—was not a function of the differences in socioeconomic status between Mexican immigrant families and native families (see second comparison in Figure 4.1). Even when, in socioeconomic terms, like was compared to like, this difference was stark. For the most part, children from Mexican immigrant families in the ECLS-K heard Spanish at home.

Learning Activities in the Family

One overriding characteristic of Mexican immigrant families is that they place incredible value on schooling. As illustrated by the Suarez-Orozcos' analysis of family narratives,[12] parents and children from Mexican immigrant families are much more likely to emphasize school achievement than those in White families. In other words, the motivations for and valuing of education are in strong supply in this population, an important piece of information that often gets lost in rhetoric and debate about Mexican immigration. What is less clear is whether Mexican immigrant parents actively translate this motivation into the kinds of active parenting behaviors that make an impact on educational success in U.S. schools. In these schools readiness is key, and so parents have to do things *before* school to get their kids ready *for* school, things such as reading or projects that forecast what will be done in school.

We know that Latino/a parents in general tend to be less likely to engage in various home learning activities than parents of other races or ethnicities, despite the value that they place on education and their strong beliefs that educational success is the key to future success.[13] Whether within this larger population Mexican immigrant families follow the same pattern has not been effectively established. Certainly, what we know about these families suggests that they will. Educational attainment is the primary factor in whether parents structure learning activities for their children, and we know that Mexican immigrant parents are, by far, less educated than other parents. We also know that Mexican immigrant parents often have greater time constraints than other parents because of their work and other responsibilities,[14] and, to the extent that home learning activities take time and effort, these time constraints may factor into parenting. Last, we know that, almost by definition, Mexican immigrant parents have less familiarity with the U.S. educational system than other parents who actually came up through this system themselves, which implies that they may know less about the importance of home learning activities for entry into and success in this system.

These expectations were, for the most part, born out in the ECLS-K sample. In the fall semester of kindergarten, parents reported how often they did various learning activities with their children, such as working with art, exploring nature, and building things. I used these reports to create a scale of home learn-

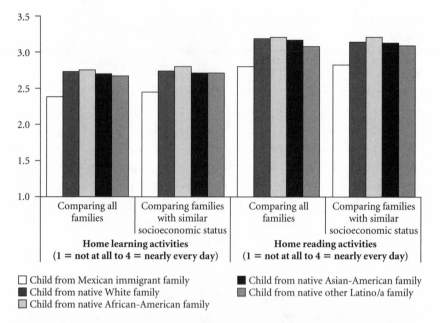

Figure 4.2 Predicted level of home activities of average child in five populations

ing activities that ranged from a high of 4 to a low of 1. Parents at the high end did these things, at least some of them, every day, and parents at the low end did not engage in any such activities at all. At the same time, parents also reported how often they read books or looked at picture books with their children, which I used to create a similar 4-point scale of home reading activities.

The predicted levels of home learning and reading activities are presented in Figure 4.2 (see Table A8 in the Appendix for the full results of these two sets of comparisons). The story is a relatively simple one. Regardless of demographic characteristics or socioeconomic status, Mexican immigrant parents were less likely to engage in either of the two learning activities at home at the start of kindergarten than were parents in the four native racial or ethnic populations. In fact, these four other populations had fairly similar rates of these home activities. Mexican immigrant families were, to borrow a statistical term, the outliers, meaning that they were the ones who looked different from the rest.

Parental Involvement at School

The final parenting behavior considered in this study moves us outside the home and into the school, specifically, the involvement of parents at their children's schools in the form of volunteering, communication, and visits. This parenting behavior is one of the most commonly studied aspects of the home-school partnership, especially in sociology, and it has become a major focal point of school policies across the nation.[15]

A good deal of evidence has documented that less educated parents are less likely to be involved in such activities than college-educated parents and that, above and beyond parents' educational attainment, racial or ethnic minority parents are also less likely than their White counterparts to actively participate in the goings-on of the school. Three powerful factors explain these trends, the first two somewhat poignant and the last infuriating. First, less educated parents are simply less knowledgeable about schools, and, as a result, either do not know how important their involvement can be for their children's success or else feel less comfortable in the school setting, especially in interactions with teachers and other parents. Second, minority parents, especially Latino/a and African-American parents, often feel a sense of mistrust regarding their children's schools and the people who run them. In some ways the historical mistreatment of minority students in U.S. schools has made them wary of getting too involved. Third, schools actively and passively discourage less educated parents and minority parents from getting involved in school either because they feel such involvement is bothersome or simply because the business of schools runs smoother without parents getting too involved, and these parents are the easiest to ignore.[16]

These general trends seem to apply directly to the Mexican immigrant experience. Indeed, Mexican immigrant parents are less involved in the day-to-day goings-on of school and less visible in their children's schools no matter what their involvement patterns look like outside the school.[17] Added to these reasons is the lower proficiency in English among these parents, which is a major hindrance in dealing with teachers and communicating in schools in the United States, especially considering the relatively halfhearted attempts of most schools to employ language outreach.

Indeed, in the ECLS-K sample Mexican immigrant parents and African-American parents were less involved at their children's schools than native parents, as revealed by the predicted amounts of parental involvement (a count of how many of seven involvement activities, such as volunteering or attending school events, parents had undertaken since the start of kindergarten) depicted in Figure 4.3 (see Table A7 in the Appendix for the full results of the comparisons used to estimate these amounts). Holding socioeconomic status constant

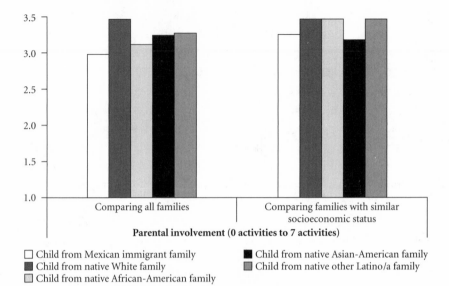

Figure 4.3 Predicted level of parental involvement at school of average child in five populations

across families did away with most of the African-American disadvantage, but it did not reduce the relative disparity between Mexican immigrant parents and native parents, with one exception. Once family socioeconomic characteristics were taken into account (second comparison in Figure 4.3), all parents with origins in Latin America (Mexican immigrant and other Latinos/as) had lower levels of parental involvement at their children's schools than their native White, African-American, and Asian-American counterparts. In this case, therefore, rates of parental involvement were more closely related to ethnicity than to socioeconomic status.

Home Summary

Past research has documented that Mexican immigrant parents really care about education and want their children to do well in school, but my study has revealed that this highly positive feature of Mexican immigrant families does not necessarily translate into certain active parenting strategies that work well in the U.S. educational system. Before and during their children's transition into elementary school, Mexican immigrant parents are less likely to construct home learning and reading activities for their children or to become active participants at their children's schools. Moreover, they are less likely to speak English to their children on a regular basis. For the most part these comparisons, all of them, hold when comparing Mexican immigrant families to native Whites or to native minority families.

Thus one aspect of the family life of children from Mexican immigrant families may place them at risk for less successful entries into elementary school, even if these children enjoy many other valuable social and emotional resources in their families and even if the active parenting processes at work in these families would be more promotive of school success in Mexico. The point is that in U.S. schools the learning strategies of Mexican immigrant families do not fit as well with school strategies.

The Child Care Market Serving Mexican Immigrant Families

Historically, the first year of elementary school has marked a major transition event in the lives of American children. More than just the advent of formal education, it is also a highly symbolic event: the full-scale movement of children from the private sphere of family life to the public sphere of societal institutions, their introduction to the way that American society works for adults.[18] Yet the traditional symbolism of this transition is itself undergoing transition in the modern era. Changes in family, work, economic, and political arenas have drastically increased the entry of women, including mothers, into the paid labor force and have fundamentally altered marital arrangements. With these changes have come changes in how children are introduced to the public sphere. Today, the *norm* in the United States is for children to spend time in the informal system of early child care before they enter the formal system of schooling.[19] In other words, elementary school is typically the second stop in the transition out of the home for American children.

What is the significance of this second stop? In general, it means that walking through the schoolhouse doors on the first day of elementary school is not the new, unknown experience that it once was. Many children have spent a good deal of time in organized settings, often engaging in formal educational curricula in these settings. Many children have learned how to spend long periods of the day away from home. Many children are used to having nonparental authority figures in charge of them and know how to interact with large groups of other children. Of course, many children also still follow the traditional route of moving directly from the home to the school. In short, all of this new variability in children's movement into public life leads to variability in how well children are equipped for school life.[20] Importantly, this variability may be closely linked to Mexican immigrant status.

If early child care experiences are a springboard into the transition to elementary school, then we should consider the different types of early child care that are typically found in American society. First, home-based child care encompasses two distinct categories: sole parental care, which is self-explanatory; and nonparental care, which refers to relatives (e.g., grandparents) or nonrelatives (e.g., babysitters) caring for children, often in groups, in the children's homes or in the caregivers' homes before the start of elementary school. Second, center-based care always occurs outside the home. Centers are typically accredited and staffed by trained personnel; in general, they serve large numbers of children organized into age-graded groups. Some centers—preschools or nursery schools—are specifically education focused.[21]

These various arrangements represent qualitatively different environments for children in the years leading up to elementary school and, as such, have the potential to differentiate children in their school readiness. Ample evidence suggests that children who spend more time in high-quality center-based care tend to do better academically when they enter elementary school. The reason is that good centers, especially preschools, focus on intellectual development and the cultivation of academic skills, such as reading and number sense, as part of formalized, structured curricula overseen by educated staff members. Not surprisingly, then, center-based care is the overwhelming preference for most parents who need some help with child care.[22] Home-based child care, including sole parental care, does not seem to have these direct observable effects on school readiness in the strict academic sense.

Given this evidence, one could conclude that child populations in which rates of center-based care are high will be more school ready than those in which it is low. This conclusion may be true in general, but it might not hold when focusing specifically on children from Mexican immigrant families. The complicating factor here is that more home-based care, especially sole parental care, is also associated with slightly better behavioral adjustment among children than center-based care for many reasons, including the low adult:child ratio in these settings.[23] This is an important issue to consider because, for children from Mexican immigrant families, the start of elementary school is more than just the advent of formal schooling or of public life. For most, it is their large-scale introduction to American life and culture.[24] In this potentially jarring transition, socioemotional adjustment and behavior may be a "smoothing" factor, one that has an impact on their early academic experiences above and beyond their actual school readiness.

The main point here is that children from Mexican immigrant families will demonstrate differential rates of early learning if they congregate in, or are seg-regated in, different sectors of the early child care market. The sectors in which they are found will have implications, both positive and negative, for how they eventually do when they make the transition into formal schooling.

Different Forms of Early Child Care

As with so many of the topics that I cover in this book, early child care has been studied extensively by social and behavioral scientists and has been the sub-ject of endless public discussions without ever being connected to immigration from Mexico. For example, the NICHD Early Child Care Research Network, of which I recently became a member, has conducted the most comprehensive, extensive study of child care in U.S. history, covering almost two decades at a cost of more than $100 million, but the many findings of this network say noth-ing about children from Mexican immigrant families, the fastest growing child population in the United States. Likewise, the so-called child care wars—pub-lic, often political, debates about the potential harm that extensive nonparental child care is doing to American children—has been waging for decades, but it has rarely, if ever, included the opinions of or opinions about Mexican im-migrant families.

Once again, therefore, we have to build our expectations of where in the early child care market children from Mexican immigrant families will be con-gregated based on research on related subjects. What this related evidence sug-gests is that children from Mexican immigrant families will be overrepresented in home-based care (especially sole parental care) and underrepresented in center-based care (especially preschool). Let me backtrack for a bit to lay out three reasons for how I arrived at this conclusion. First, because Mexican im-migrant families tend to be poorer than other families, the greater expense of center-based care may be prohibitive. Second, the lower familiarity that Mexi-can immigrant parents, as newcomers, have with how child care works in the United States may also limit their ability to access more public child care set-tings. Third, the more communal nature of Mexican-origin neighborhoods and kin networks may be an informal service sector for things such as child care, creating more accessible and affordable home-based child care arrange-ments.[25] Finally, and most important, we do know that immigrant families in general are more likely to rely on home-based child care arrangements, as are Mexican-American families, regardless of immigrant status.[26]

Does this suggested pattern actually reflect the experiences of Mexican immigrant families? To answer this question, I worked with parents' reports in the ECLS-K about the various child care arrangements they had used in the year before their children entered kindergarten. Only 16% of parents reported that they had been the sole caregiver for their children, and an additional 22% said that their children had been cared for, at least part-time, by relatives or by nonrelatives in single-child or small group settings. Alternatively, fully 39% of parents reported that their children had been enrolled in day care centers for at least some part of the year before kindergarten, most of whom specifically designated these arrangements as preschools.

For each of these dimensions of early child care, I compared children in that type to all other children, including children in the other three types of child care and children in other nonparental child care arrangements not covered by these three types. Thus the proper comparison is, for example, between children in preschool versus children not in preschool. The full results of these comparisons are contained in Table A9 and Table A10 in the Appendix. As in previous chapters, I have boiled down these complicated results into a more usable form for readers less interested in the statistical mechanisms that I used to arrive at them.

Table 4.1 shows a basic comparison of the average White and the average non-White child in each type of child care arrangement, first comparing children from families of varying socioeconomic circumstances and second comparing children from families of similar socioeconomic circumstances. Children from Mexican immigrant families were much more likely to be solely in parental care than native White children. Actually, they were much more likely to be solely in parental care than children from any native racial or ethnic population, especially African-American children. A large chunk of these differences in parental care was related to the lower socioeconomic status of Mexican immigrant families relative to other families. Because Mexican immigrant parents had lower rates of educational attainment and employment (mothers in particular) and because they were poorer, they had less need for or means for nonparental child care. Once these socioeconomic factors were taken into account, these families looked more like other families. In fact, the differences between Mexican immigrant families and Latino/a and Asian-American families in the use of sole parental care disappeared when Mexican immigrant families were compared to other families with similar socioeconomic circumstances.

The story was slightly different for the other form of home-based child care. Yes, children from Mexican immigrant families had lower odds of being

Table 4.1 Comparison of Early Child Care Arrangements Between the Average
Native White Child and Children from Different Minority Populations

Child Care Arrangement	Comparing All Families	Comparing Families with Similar Socioeconomic Status
Average child from Mexican immigrant family		
More likely to be in _____ than average child from native White family	Parental care	Parental care Nonparental/home-based
Less likely to be in _____ than average child from native White family	Nonparental/home-based Preschool Day care center	Preschool Day care center
Average child from native African-American family		
More likely to be in _____ than average child from native White family	Day care center	
Less likely to be in _____ than average child from native White family	Parental care Preschool	Parental care Nonparental/home-based Preschool
Average child from native Asian-American family		
More likely to be in _____ than average child from native White family	Parental care	Parental care
Less likely to be in _____ than average child from native White family	Preschool Day care center	Preschool Day care center
Average child from native other Latino/a family		
More likely to be in _____ than average child from native White family	Parental care	Parental care
Less likely to be in _____ than average child from native White family	Preschool	Preschool

in nonparental home-based child care than native White children, or any other
native children for that matter, but these differences were within the margin of
error in only one case—the comparison of children from Mexican immigrant
families to their other Latino/a peers. At first glance, the other Latino/a children
were the most likely to be in home-based but not parental care. Adding family socioeconomic characteristics to the mix, however, revealed a completely
different situation. When families were compared to other families of similar
socioeconomic status, children from Mexican immigrant families and other

Latino/a children were, together, the most likely to be in nonparental home-based child care of all the different populations considered.

The story was much simpler for center-based care. Regardless of family socioeconomic characteristics, children from Mexican immigrant families had, by far, the lowest rate of enrollment in preschool of all racial and ethnic populations. Moreover, they were far less likely to be found in day care centers than White, African-American, and Asian-American children, again regardless of socioeconomic status. They were also less likely than other Latino/a children in general to be in day care centers in the year before kindergarten, but they were roughly equal to other Latino/as of similar socioeconomic status in such enrollment.

Early Child Care Summary

If the secular trend in the United States is toward early child care as an intermediate step in the transition of children from the home to the school, then children from Mexican immigrant families are bucking this trend. More than any other racial or ethnic population, children from Mexican immigrant families tended to be cared for at home by their parents in the years before the start of school. When not at home with their parents, they tended to be in other forms of home-based care, such as being watched by relatives, but they were unlikely—at least compared to other children—to be in more organized, center-based settings of nonparental child care. Most striking, these children, by and large, did *not* attend preschool.

Given what we already know about the implications of different early child care arrangements for school readiness, these patterns would seem to suggest that children from Mexican immigrant families will have a harder time adapting to the academic demands and routines of elementary school. Yet, as I pointed out earlier in this chapter, our general knowledge about early child care may not overlay so neatly onto the Mexican immigrant experience. Thus, determining which is more important for the early learning of children from Mexican immigrant families—the potential cognitive benefits of center-based care or the socioemotional benefits of home-based care—is what is known in science as an empirical question. Put simply, we have to ask the question without knowing the answer.

Schools Serving Children from Mexican Immigrant Families

In the United States the concept of equality of opportunity has become deeply ingrained in the national consciousness. In fact, the so-called founder of American education, Horace Mann of Massachusetts, made a mantra out of claiming repeatedly in the nineteenth century that equality of opportunity was the bedrock of the nascent public education system that was just beginning to take hold as the centerpiece of the great American experiment. The general principle of equality of opportunity was the same then as it is now: All children, no matter what their family background, demographic status, or position in society, could go to school in the United States and, through educational attainment, eventually better their lot in life. By giving all children the same opportunity to attend school, therefore, the United States gave them all the same opportunity to pursue long-term success. This equality of opportunity was thought to be essential to ensuring that the great demographic diversity in this new and growing country—a potent and potentially combustible mix of races, ethnic groups, and classes constantly refueled by immigration—did not translate into massive, intransigent inequality.

That this concept of equality of opportunity was and is a worthy goal is not really debatable, but whether this concept has ever become reality in the United States is. Back then, of course, many children were not allowed in school at all. Today, every child has the right to go to school, but they do not have the right to go to good schools. As the pigs decreed in Orwell's *Animal Farm*, all are born equal, but some are born more equal than others. Indeed, some sectors of the U.S. population are served by schools that are not good (when speaking charitably) or even awful (when speaking bluntly), whereas other children attend schools with the best of everything available to them.[27] The potential consequences of this inequality of opportunity have been well documented by sociologists, psychologists, economists, and other educational researchers, and the findings of this research will surprise no one. Two children who spend twelve years in starkly different learning environments—one marked by disorganization, substandard materials, and poor teaching and the other marked by an abundance of resources, safety, and enriched curricula—generally wind up with quite different positions and prospects in life as they transition into adulthood. A lot goes into this difference, including concomitant neighborhood and community inequalities, but the disparate opportunities that they face year in and year out in their respective sectors of the public education system certainly play a major role.[28]

Bringing this topic back to the focus of this book, Mexican immigrants make up one of the most socioeconomically disadvantaged populations in the United States, and so they have the most to gain by capitalizing on the opportunity for public education to garner much needed academic credentials—credentials that, collectively, will ultimately promote the socioeconomic prospects of the Mexican-American population as a whole. Yet this theoretical process will bear out in reality in only one case: if equality of opportunity means that children from Mexican immigrant families and native White children have equal access to good schools, not just equal access to schools in general. That is an "if" that needs to be investigated. Given the cumulative nature of education, if children from Mexican immigrant families enter the U.S. educational system through more problematic elementary schools, then they will likely demonstrate truncated rates of educational attainment in the long run, leaving intact the overall inequality in the United States that favors other groups over the growing Mexican-origin population.

Thus, in order to assess this possibility, we need to first determine whether children from Mexican immigrant families attend more problematic elementary schools than their peers from native racial and ethnic populations. Certainly, some evidence suggests that they do, which makes sense considering what we know about the neighborhood and community segregation of the Mexican-origin population.[29] These apparent patterns of inequality of opportunity, however, are tangled up with the complex socioeconomic differences that go hand in hand with race and ethnicity in the United States. Disentangling the two is a crucial step in figuring out how best to help children from Mexican immigrant families.

I should note that this line of research on the school enrollment patterns of Mexican immigrant children is something that I earlier tackled in a 2005 article in *American Educational Research Journal*.[30] I have adapted the basic framework of that earlier study of school segregation for the purposes of this book.

School Context

Fortunately, the ECLS-K contains a wealth of information about schools. In fact, it contains almost too much information, which makes choosing what to study a challenging task. I decided to focus on three general categories of school characteristics that tend to garner the most attention from scientific researchers and that have been most closely linked to academic performance and educational attainment: school structure (how the school is formally organized), composition (what types of children attend the school), and climate (what the general setting and atmosphere of the school is like). I then examined two specific indicators of school context within each of these three general categories. All these school context characteristics referred to the school in which children attended first grade. Unlike in all previous chapters, therefore, this developmental context was measured in the year in which children made the transition to first grade and not the year preceding this transition. This shift in time span was necessary to gauge the actual context in which math learning was occurring rather than the context (or domain) setting the foundation for this learning.

For school structure the principal of each school estimated the number of students enrolled in that school on a 5-point scale on which schools with fewer than 150 students scored a 1 and schools with more than 750 students scored a 5. This estimate allowed me to measure school size. Teachers in each school reported the number of years that they had taught in their current schools and in first grade. I did a little work with these two reports (see Appendix), producing a measure of low teacher experience that ran from 0 to 9.2. For composition I calculated the percentage of the student body of each school that belonged to a racial or ethnic minority population and that fell below the federal poverty line. Finally, for climate I drew heavily on previous work with the ECLS-K by Valerie Lee and David Burkham[31]—averaging principal reports about the extent of seven problems present in the neighborhoods surrounding their schools (e.g., excessive litter, public drinking, violent crimes, vacant buildings) to create a 4-point scale for disorganized community location and then counting the number of safety problems reported by principals within each school (e.g., things being taken, physical attacks) to create a 3-point scale of school safety problems.

With these six school characteristics, I wanted to assess whether children from Mexican immigrant families were overrepresented in schools that placed their early learning and social psychological adjustment at risk and, again, whether any such overrepresentation was actually a function of their family socioeconomic characteristics rather than their immigrant status. To do so, I worked with propensity scores. The Appendix contains a complete description of propensity score techniques for those readers who want to know more about this method, but I would like to make a few general comments about these techniques here.

Propensity scores catalog a series of characteristics into a single index. This index can be used to efficiently and simply match children who share similar characteristics. For example, a major focus of this study, as just mentioned, is the possibility that Mexican immigrant status is tangled up with family socioeconomic characteristics, and propensity scores offer a way to do a little disentangling. By cataloging the family socioeconomic characteristics that go along with Mexican immigrant status into one index (the propensity score), I can then compare children from Mexican immigrant families to those children from other racial and ethnic populations with a similar family socioeconomic profile by matching them on a single propensity score rather than by matching them on several separate family socioeconomic characteristics. This is exactly what I did to investigate racial and ethnic differences in school enrollment patterns.

School Structure, Composition, and Climate

Actually, to be specific, I created *two* propensity scores, the first one being a single index cataloging the set of basic demographic characteristics (e.g., sex, age, immigrant status, region, and urbanicity) used so often already, and the second one being a single index cataloging these control variables *plus* the full set of family socioeconomic variables (e.g., family socioeconomic status, family poverty, family structure, maternal employment, paternal employment). I then used both propensity scores to compare children from Mexican immigrant families to children from native racial or ethnic populations on school enrollment. For example, matching children from Mexican immigrant families to their native White peers on the first propensity score allowed me to assess Mexican-White differences in school enrollment regardless of family socioeconomic characteristics, and matching them on the second propensity score allowed me to assess the same differences when family socioeconomic characteristics were held constant.

Figure 4.4 contains the results of these comparisons for the two aspects of school structure (Table A11 in the Appendix contains the full results of these comparisons). On average, children from Mexican immigrant families attended bigger schools than native White children, as evidenced by the higher average school size score for the Mexican immigrant children (white bar in Figure 4.4) compared to the White children (black bar). This basic Mexican-White difference did not go away when children from Mexican immigrant families (white bar) were compared only to White children whose families had similar socioeconomic profiles (gray bar). The exact same pattern was seen for the second aspect of school structure. On average, the teachers of children from Mexican immigrant families had fewer years of training and experience than those who taught White children, even White children who shared their same family background.

Turning to school composition, Figure 4.5 contains the same comparisons

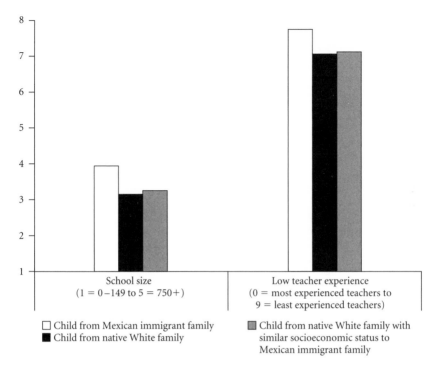

Figure 4.4 Predicted school structural characteristics of average child in different populations

for the proportion of the student body from a racial or ethnic minority and in poverty. Essentially, we see the same pattern as described in Figure 4.4. Comparing children from Mexican immigrant families to all native White children reveals an enormous difference in the rates of attendance at racially and economically segregated schools. When comparing children from Mexican immigrant families to White children who were similar to them in terms of their families' socioeconomic characteristics, we see a smaller but still sizable difference in these rates of attendance.

Figure 4.6 shows more of the same for school climate. Children from Mexican immigrant families were overrepresented in schools situated in disorganized (e.g., high-crime) communities relative to native White children in general and relative to those with similar family socioeconomic profiles. The one exception to this basic rule concerns school safety problems. In general, children from Mexican immigrant families attended less safe schools than Whites, but this difference disappeared when their enrollment patterns were compared only to

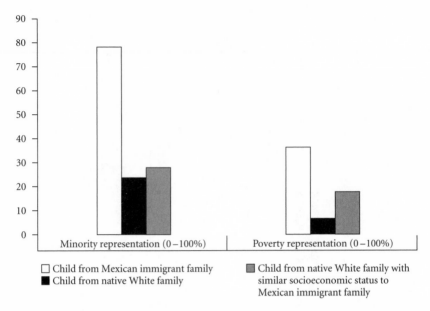

Figure 4.5 Predicted school compositional characteristics of average child in different populations

White children with similar family circumstances. In this one case, therefore, what appeared to be an inequality of opportunity related to immigrant status was actually one related to family socioeconomic status. In all other cases this inequality appeared to be a direct function of immigrant status.

These same sets of school enrollment comparisons were made for children from Mexican immigrant families versus native African-American children, Asian-American children, and other Latino/a children. The results of these comparisons were almost identical to the Mexican-White differences just described. In fact, they were so similar that describing the few exceptions found in these other comparisons is far easier than presenting the results of these comparisons in graphical form, as I did for the Mexican-White comparison. For all three of these other comparisons, the exception involved safety problems in schools. First, African-American children attended less safe schools than children from Mexican immigrant families, on average, and this difference persisted whether children were compared only to others from similar family socioeconomic backgrounds or not. This was the one case in which children from Mexican immigrant families appeared to fare better in an aspect of school enrollment than a native population. Second, the schools in which children

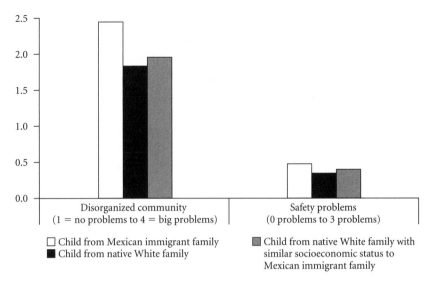

Figure 4.6 Predicted school climate characteristics of average child in different populations

from Mexican immigrant families were enrolled were no more or no less unsafe than those in which Asian-American or other Latino/a children were enrolled, whether socioeconomic characteristics were taken into account or not.

School Summary

This analysis of equality of opportunity to learn presents quite a stark picture for children from Mexican immigrant families. The overwhelming weight of this evidence demonstrates that Mexican immigrant children attend different schools than their peers from other racial or ethnic populations do, and for the most part *different* means *worse*. In short, when parents immigrated to the United States from Mexico, their children started their careers in the U.S. educational system in schools that were bigger, more segregated, staffed by less experienced teachers, and housed in more problematic neighborhoods than other children their age, even if these schools did not differ in safety. Moreover, this apparent pattern of the strict segregation of children from Mexican immigrant families was not merely a function of the socioeconomic segregation of their schools or of their larger communities. Thus these children had equal access to the educational system, but only in the most hairsplitting definition of equality of opportunity.

What are the implications of this early inequality of opportunity? Certainly, prior scientific research on school effects on academic performance and educational attainment suggests that these school enrollment patterns place children from Mexican immigrant families at risk at the start of their educational careers.[32] In the next chapter of this book—in which I present the results of an in-depth investigation of how the various aspects of the focal developmental domains and contexts, including schools, contribute to early learning and early inequalities in learning—I determine whether this "suggestion" is in fact reality.

5 The High Stakes of Early Learning in Math

SO FAR, I have given evidence that children from Mexican immigrant families differ from their peers in many aspects of the developmental process—both how and where development unfolds. Why should you care about these differences? The answer to this question is pretty simple. Not only are these differences important markers of inequality in their own right, but they also have potential to translate into corresponding differences in early learning. This potential is the main focus of this chapter.

Entry-Level Math Learning

In describing and discussing various facets of child development so far in this book, I have separated out several aspects of the children themselves as well as several aspects of their living environments. This is what social and behavioral scientists often do when they conduct research on child development. They focus intently on specific, manageable pieces of the child, say, his or her health or education, in an in-depth way and then treat the other pieces of the child as "noise" in the equation. Yet all of us who have been children or who have raised children (and that is everyone, isn't it?) knows that these little people, each of them, are complex, multidimensional, internally contradictory bundles of characteristics, traits, behaviors, and experiences lived in diverse settings. In any given child some of these pieces are good, some bad; some cause for concern, others for praise. How all these pieces come together is what identifies the unique situation and life prospects of each child. Taking in the "whole child," therefore, is crucial to understanding and serving that child.

Moving up from the level of the individual child to the level of child populations, this whole-child philosophy also provides a highly valuable tool for looking at educational inequalities related to race or ethnicity, immigration, and other important and timely aspects of U.S. demography. The school transition model formulated by Karl Alexander and Doris Entwisle that served as the basic blueprint of this study was steeped in this philosophy. As you may recall from Chapter 1, the school transition model strongly asserts that such inequalities are rooted in the general configuration of circumstances that make up the lives of children from different segments of the U.S. population. That lesson is a good one. No one can ever capture every single aspect of the whole child, which spans DNA to the basic layout of the universe after all, but we can and should start moving in the direction of more holistic treatments of children in general and of young students in the educational system in particular—looking inside and outside the child, looking inside and outside the school, all at the same time.

Taking the whole child into account, however, is not as straightforward as it may seem, and different researchers take different approaches to this task. In this book I attempt a more holistic perspective by comparing and contrasting several aspects of children's lives—who they know, where they are, how they think and feel, and what they do—and the contributions of each of these aspects to early learning. In other words, I recognize that many different things can promote or hinder early learning, that some may be stronger than others, that some may overlap with others, and that some may work through others. Rather than focusing on any one piece of the child in isolation, therefore, I attempt to tease apart and then capture the relative contributions of different pieces of the child to experiences in math, the school curriculum that is so closely related to educational and socioeconomic attainment in the long run.[1]

To evaluate the contributions of family socioeconomic circumstances as well as various domains and contexts of child development to math learning during the transition to elementary school, I first assessed the degree to which each of these sets of factors was connected to math learning when they were examined one at a time. I then made the same assessment when they were examined together. The first assessment indicated what increase or decrease in math learning could conceivably result from a change in a particular set of factors. The second assessment allowed the comparison of different sets of factors to determine which would most likely have the biggest impact on math learning if manipulated. To elaborate a little more, we find that the first piece of information will be useful if policymakers want to target a specific intervention strategy (e.g., child care)—it will tell them what they might expect to accomplish. The second piece of information will be useful if policymakers are trying to decide what kind of intervention strategy to target (e.g., child care or school context)—it will tell them the most promising route to take. In this way we can identify tools that combine effectiveness and "doability."

Differences in Math Learning at First Glance

The first step in this endeavor is to establish that children from Mexican immigrant families do start out their elementary school careers with lower rates of learning in math than their classmates and peers. As described in Chapter 2, the children in the ECLS-K were regularly given standardized tests in math. One might ask how a math test for young children might look. Essentially, these tests asked children to identify numbers, do basic counts, and compute simple operations (e.g., addition), among other things. These tests grew progressively more difficult with each semester and year. After doing some work with children's raw answers on these tests, the statisticians at the NCES produced basic math scores for each child that were directly comparable from child to child and from year to year for each individual child (refer to the Appendix for a more detailed discussion of these scores).

The statistical analysis that I performed on these math test scores allowed me to generate the predicted score on this math test of the average child in each population of interest, where average refers to sex, age, immigrant status, region, and urbanicity. As seen in Table 5.1, the average child from a Mexican immigrant family did indeed score lower on the math test in the spring

Table 5.1 Predicted Math Scores and Math Score Differentials in First Grade for the Average Child in Each Population

Population	Predicted Score[a]	Point Differential vs. Mexican Immigrant
Child from Mexican immigrant family	48.71	—
Child from native White family	58.52	−9.81
Child from native African-American family	48.83	−0.12
Child from native Asian-American family	57.29	−8.58
Child from native Latino/a family	51.95	−3.24

[a] Controlling only for sex, age, region, and urbanicity.

semester of first grade than the average child from the native race or ethnic populations (see Table A12 in the Appendix for the complete results that generated these predicted scores). Actually, the difference between Mexican-origin and African-American children was not a statistically significant one, but all other differences were. On average, children from Mexican immigrant families scored almost 10 points lower on this test than similar White children, almost 9 points lower than similar Asian-American children, and just over 3 points lower than other Latino/a children. In other words, children from Mexican immigrant families start this absolutely crucial curriculum already at a disadvantage.

The second column in Table 5.1 gives us the basic point differentials between children from Mexican immigrant families and their peers. These differentials provide the reference point to all subsequent comparisons in my discussion of first-grade math learning. In other words, every time I take into account a developmental domain or context, I compare the point differentials generated from that analysis to these initial point differentials in Table 5.1. For this reason, I refer to these initial point differentials as the "differences at first glance."

After calculating these differences at first glance, in the second step I generated new predicted math scores that took into account racial/ethnic and immigration-related differences in family socioeconomic circumstances (in technical terms, I added the socioeconomic factors to the model predicting first-grade math score). Comparing the point differentials from this step to the differences at first glance allowed me to evaluate the degree to which differences in first-grade math learning related to Mexican immigrant status resulted from corresponding differences in family socioeconomic circumstances. The third step was to take out the family socioeconomic factors, replace them with the four health factors representing the first developmental domain, and then compare the point differentials that took health into account to the differences at first glance. This step was repeated for all the domains and contexts up to the eighth step, in which the six school factors were the only factors assessed in relation to math learning (except the control variables of course) and in which the point differentials revealed by this assessment were compared to the differences at first glance. The final modeling step assessed all the socioeconomic, developmental domain, and developmental context factors at the same time.

What should be clear by now is that I am most interested in how point differentials between children from Mexican immigrant families and native children changed in relation to family socioeconomic circumstances, various developmental domains, and developmental contexts. Of course, change encompasses two directions: point differentials that decrease and point differentials that increase. Each direction tells a different story.

To explain what a decrease in point differentials represents, I use the example of physical health. If taking health into account *reduces* differences in math learning at first glance, then I can conclude that health is a risk factor for the early learning of children from Mexican immigrant families—their health places these children at risk for lower levels of early learning in math relative to native children. Specifically, poor health constrains the learning of children from Mexican immigrant families, and so taking this disadvantage into account—by comparing these children to others who have similarly poor health—washes out the previously observed learning difference related to this disadvantage. If so, then the early learning of children from Mexican immigrant families would likely benefit from intervention that improves their health.

To explain what a decrease in point differentials represents, I use the example of self-regulation. If taking self-regulation into account *increases* these differences in math learning at first glance, then I can conclude that self-regulation is a protective factor—it boosts the early learning of children from Mexican immigrant families relative to native children. Specifically, self-regulation represents something that is an advantage to children from Mexican immigrant families, and so comparing children from Mexican immigrant families to native children with similarly high levels of self-regulation would actually strengthen only the previously observed learning difference related to this advantage. In other words, if not for this psychosocial advantage, children from Mexican immigrant families would be doing worse, which means that policy and intervention might work with this particular resource to help other children do better at the start of school.

To recap before diving into my actual findings, I first assessed the potential contribution of family socioeconomic circumstances, three developmental domains, and three developmental contexts to math learning in first grade independent of each other. I then assessed them all together to determine their relative contributions.

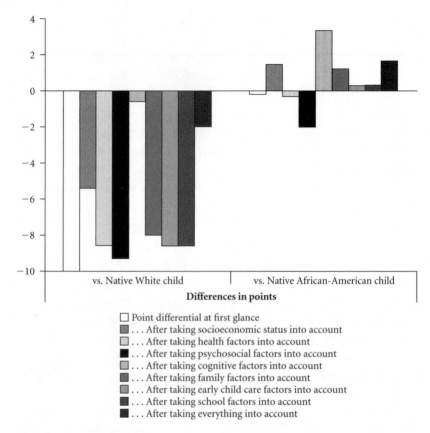

Figure 5.1 Predicted point differentials on first-grade math test for average child from Mexican immigrant family

Figures 5.1 and 5.2 present, in user-friendly form, the results of the comparison of differences in math learning at first glance to differences that take these various sets of factors into account. Figure 5.1 contains the results comparing children from Mexican immigrant families to their native White and African-American peers. Figure 5.2 contains the results comparing children from Mexican immigrant families to their native Asian-American and other Latino/a peers. In both figures a bar that extends downward from the center line indicates a point differential favoring the comparison racial or ethnic population, and a bar that extends upward from this center line indicates a point differential favoring children from Mexican immigrant families. Tables A12 and A13 in the Appendix contain the complete results that generated these predicted point differentials.

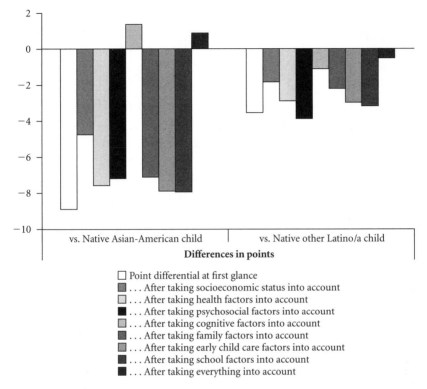

Figure 5.2 Predicted point differentials on first-grade math test for average child from Mexican immigrant family

Considering Math Learning in Relation to Family Socioeconomic Characteristics

Once the family socioeconomic factors were held constant across populations, the point differentials between children from Mexican immigrant families and native White, Asian-American, and other Latino/a children seen at first glance were each cut approximately in half. Thus, if children from Mexican immigrant families had the same basic family socioeconomic profile as White children, they would still be lagging behind in early math learning but at a much lower level than in the current reality. The same would be true if Asian-American or other Latino/a children were the comparison. On the other hand, taking family socioeconomic characteristics into account actually increased the average point differential between Mexican-origin and African-American children from virtually zero to about one and a half points (note the second bar extending upward from the center line in the African-American panel of Figure 5.1). Thus, if children from Mexican immigrant families had the same basic family socioeconomic profile as African-American children, they would likely outperform them in math.

Considering Math Learning in Relation to Developmental Domains

Family socioeconomic status, of course, is at the heart of many racial/ethnic and immigration-related differences in education, health, and other domains across life stages. This much has been proven repeatedly by social scientists. Yet family socioeconomic background is not the final word in this debate. The other aspects of children's lives and environments deserve attention. In shifting attention to these other aspects, I begin with the three developmental domains that have been covered so far in this book.

Health was the first developmental domain of interest. I took out family socioeconomic circumstances for the moment and, in their place, assessed the various health factors. All four aspects of poor health predicted lower math learning in first grade, with internalizing symptoms the most important of the four. Compared to the differences at first glance, holding health profiles equal across populations reduced the Mexican-White differential and the Mexican/Asian-American differential by just about one and a fourth points and reduced the Mexican-Latino/a differential by slightly more than one point.

Recall from Chapter 3, however, that children from Mexican immigrant families generally had poorer physical health but better mental health than their native peers, which suggests that these two aspects of health might have different, actually opposite, effects on the *relative* math learning of children from Mexican immigrant families. Consequently, I redid these analyses, looking at physical health only and then at mental health only. Essentially, the positive role of their better mental health canceled out a good deal of the negative role of the Mexican immigrant children's poorer physical health. In other words, the point differential would generally be much smaller than the differences at first glance if physical health were held constant between populations (because this dimension of health was a disadvantage for children from Mexican immigrant families) and generally greater than the differences at first glance if mental health was held constant (because this dimension of health was an advantage for these children). Thus health was an important factor in inequalities in early math learning.

As for the psychosocial domain, I replaced the four health factors in my investigation with self-regulation and social competence and again made the comparison to the differences at first glance. Both strongly predicted higher rates of math learning in first grade, with self-regulation the more important of the two. The average point differential between children from Mexican immigrant families and native White children did not change much compared to the differences at first glance when these two aspects of psychosocial development were taken into account. In fact, the differential was reduced by less than half a point. This pattern, however, did not extend to the other comparisons. Accounting for differences in these psychosocial factors reduced the differential between Mexican-origin and native Asian-American children by about one and a half points. Doing so actually increased the differential between children from Mexican immigrant families and the two native populations (1.5 points vs. African-American children, 0.5 point vs. other Latino/as). Thus psychosocial development played an important role in inequalities in early math learning between *minority* child populations.

To incorporate population differences in cognitive development into this assessment of math learning in first grade, I replaced the two psychosocial factors with low English proficiency and math test score at the start of kindergarten, the latter an attempt to capture the math skills that children bring into their first classroom experiences. Both factors predicted math learning in the first grade, with low proficiency associated with lower rates of math learning and initial level of math skills, as expected, strongly associated with later math learning.

In the comparison of children with similar preschool cognitive skills, the point differentials observed at first glance between children from Mexican immigrant families and their native White and other Latino/a peers shrunk to next to nothing. At the same time, the observed point differentials between these children and their native African-American and Asian-American peers actually reversed, now favoring children from Mexican immigrant families. In other words, children from Mexican immigrant families demonstrated slightly lower, but roughly the same, levels of math learning in first grade as White and other Latino/a children who began school with the same basic math and language skills, and they demonstrated slightly higher levels than their African-American and Asian-American peers who entered school with similar cognitive skills. Obviously, the cultivation of language and math proficiency *before* the entry into school is a major factor in what happens to children from different populations *after* they are in school.

Considering Math Learning in Relation to Developmental Contexts

Developmental domains are essentially dimensions of personal growth and maturation. On the other hand, developmental contexts are the physical settings in which the action in these domains plays out. The developmental contexts examined in Chapter 4 were the family, early child care, and the school. I repeated the same steps for these contexts as I just did for the developmental domains, namely, assessing changes in the point differentials in average predicted math test score between children from Mexican immigrant families and their native peers from other racial or ethnic populations associated with each context, independent of the other contexts and independent of family socioeconomic circumstances. Again, Table A12 in the Appendix contains the full results of these comparisons, and Figures 5.1 and 5.2 present these results in more user-friendly form.

Beginning with the family, I wanted to focus on aspects of family life that were directly related to education, in other words, education-focused parenting practices. In Chapter 4, I reported on racial/ethnic and immigration-related differences in family language use, home learning activities, home reading activities, and parents' involvement at their children's schools. These four factors were added to the initial model for first-grade math learning (the model that took nothing but sex, age, region, and urbanicity into account). Only home reading activities and parental involvement predicted higher rates of math learning in first grade, with parental involvement being more important.

Adding these factors to my examination of first-grade math learning reduced the initial point differential—the differences at first glance—between children from Mexican immigrant families and native White, Asian-American, and other Latino/a children by roughly 2 points. Moreover, adding these four factors increased the differential between Mexican-origin and native African-American children by about one and a half points, turning an observed math learning deficit into an advantage. Thus the types of learning enrichment that occurred in the family environment accounted for a rather sizable chunk of the lower relative math learning of children from Mexican immigrant families that appeared in our fast pass at comparing them to children from native racial or ethnic populations.

Next, the early child care factors replaced the four family factors in my consideration of math learning in first grade. All forms of center-based and home-based child care (especially preschool) predicted higher rates of math learning relative to children in parental care only. The gap in math learning between Mexican immigrant families and their native White, Asian-American, and other Latino/a peers would be reduced by about 1 point (depending on the exact comparison) if children from Mexican immigrant families had the same rates of enrollment in preschool and center care as their peers, but this gap would still exist. Although taking into account differences in nonparental child care between children from Mexican immigrant families and their native African-American peers appeared to reverse the point differential between the two (favoring African-American children at first glance, favoring Mexican-origin children in the child care model), the actual change in these differentials was well within the margin of error. Early child care, therefore, is the contextual equivalent of psychosocial development, important yet less so than other aspects of children's lives that have already been examined and discussed (e.g., health, socioeconomic circumstances).

Finally, the six school factors replaced the early child care factors as potential predictors of first-grade math learning. Enrollment in two kinds of schools (those segregated by race or ethnicity and poverty and those with safety problems) predicted lower rates of math learning during this period. Taking school context into account did reduce the point differentials on the math test between children from Mexican immigrant families and their native peers that were seen at first glance, but this reduction was not substantial and certainly did not eliminate those differences. Again, the apparent reversal in the point differential between children from Mexican immigrant families and their native African-American peers related to differences in school enrollment was not actually a statistically significant finding. My comment about early child care being a contextual equivalent of psychosocial factors, therefore, goes for school context too.

Considering Math Learning in Relation to Everything

The analyses described so far in this chapter indicate that family socioeconomic circumstances as well as each developmental domain and context play some role in math learning in the first grade. To directly compare the relative contributions of these different factors and then catalog the most and least effective targets for intervention, I considered *simultaneously* the contributions of family socioeconomic background, all three development domains, and all three developmental contexts.

Of course, the observed contributions for each of these sets of factors should change when they are considered together rather than separately. The reasons for such fluctuations are rooted in the whole child. Specifically, the different aspects of a child's life and environment overlap with one another, and, consequently, their effects on early learning are all tangled up together. For example, one of the great advantages of being socioeconomically privileged is that you can enroll your children in good schools. If so, then examining the family socioeconomic circumstances and school characteristics together would likely reduce the observed association between socioeconomic circumstances and math learning (because good schools are one channel through which socioeconomic advantages have an effect) and also would likely reduce the observed association between enrollment in well-organized schools and math learning (because this effect of good schools is masking the more powerful benefit of coming from a socioeconomically advantaged family). In this way, examining these factors together gives a better idea of what each has to offer in terms of math learning and provides a cleaner picture of the different ways that math learning can be targeted.

The final bar for each racial or ethnic comparison in Figures 5.1 and 5.2 provides the average predicted point differentials once all the socioeconomic, domain, and context factors have been taken into account (see Table A13 in the Appendix for the full results that generated these point differentials). These bars tell an interesting story.

If children from Mexican immigrant families and their native White peers were similar in their family background, health, psychosocial development, cognitive skills, home learning environment, early child care arrangements, and school enrollment, the difference between them on the first-grade math test would be much smaller (at least 7 points smaller) than it appears at first glance. Yet this difference would still exist and would still favor native White children over children from Mexican immigrant families.

On the other hand, if children from Mexican immigrant families were similar to their native Latino/a peers on these same socioeconomic, domain, and context factors, the differences between the two on the first-grade math test that were seen at first glance would all but disappear. The same would be true of children from Mexican immigrant families and their native Asian-American peers. In other words, if these children's lives were made the same, they would do about the same in math in the first grade.

Finally, if children from Mexican immigrant families were similar to their native African-American peers on the socioeconomic, domain, and context factors, the differences between the two on the first-grade math test that were seen at first glance would all shift to favor the children from Mexican immigrant families. Indeed, if such similarities did exist, children from Mexican immigrant families would outperform African-American children in first-grade math by about one and a half points.

As mentioned, these comprehensive analyses also shed light on the relative importance of each of these developmental domains and contexts in early learning in math. I adjusted all the estimates just described so that they could be directly compared in terms of their magnitude. Doing so revealed that kindergarten math test score was by far the most important predictor of first-grade math learning (no surprise there), followed by self-regulation and family socioeconomic status. The remaining predictors of first-grade math learning had smaller magnitudes and could be broken down into three basic groups. In order of magnitude, these groups were:

1. Social competence, parental involvement in education, minority representation in the school, and proportion of the school student body in poverty.
2. Internalizing symptoms, low English proficiency, and home language use.
3. Poor physical health, physical health problems, and home reading activities.

No other factor predicted first-grade math learning in any meaningful way. Some factors that were prominent in earlier considerations of math learning (e.g., externalizing symptoms) faded substantially in this comprehensive treatment because their associations with first-grade math learning were accounted for or related to other socioeconomic or developmental characteristics. Likewise, other factors that did not appear to be important initially became more prominent in this comprehensive treatment because they had initially been masked by other socioeconomic or developmental characteristics. Still, all developmental domains and contexts were represented in this list, with child care the one exception. Most forms of nonparental care were originally associated with higher math learning when viewed by themselves, but these associations were washed away by the inclusion of the cognitive factors, suggesting that nonparental care (especially center-based care) fosters math learning in elementary school by affecting preschool cognitive skills.

Entry-Level Math Summary

In first grade, children from Mexican immigrant families had lower rates of learning in math than most of their native peers, a status that posed great risk for their long-term educational and socioeconomic attainment. This math learning gap was most evident when they were compared to native White and Asian-American children and smallest when children from Mexican immigrant families were compared to native African-American children. Even at the widest point, however, these learning gaps were not huge. Yet, given the basic point of school transition research (e.g., the work of Alexander, Entwisle, Lee, Burkham, Pianta, Walsh, Cox, and others) that even the most striking demographic inequalities in educational attainment grow out of initially small differences that are compounded over the years of formal schooling, these narrow gaps are cause for great concern when dealing with a population in which levels of socioeconomic disadvantage are coupled with an exponential rate of growth.

The results presented so far suggest that these early learning gaps are malleable, responsive to adjustments in family situation and other circumstances of life. Most important, targeting entry-level cognitive skills and family socioeconomic resources would do the most to reduce these gaps, followed by education-focused family processes and good health and then, to a lesser degree, formal child care, school organization, and psychosocial skills. Separately, each set of factors could potentially be leverageable in attempts to help children from Mexican immigrant families start out on an even playing field in the math curriculum, either by eliminating Mexican-origin children's disadvantages in some of these areas or building on their already existing advantages in others. Most likely, however, interventions will be most effective if they target many or all of these factors in tandem because those factors will add to each other and channel each other. Deciphering which set of factors has the largest impact while also being the most amenable to policy intervention—in other words, the easiest to implement—will be the decisive point in these important and timely efforts.

Gains in Math Learning over Time

The *starting gate* is a term for the advent of elementary school that is used quite often in discussions of early learning, and so, naturally, I have introduced it in this book. This term brings to mind a race, and that is not unintentional.

In many ways the educational system is just that, a race. One often hears the professional baseball season described as "a marathon, not a sprint," and the race that is the educational system also fits this description. It is one long, demanding, meandering race. So many runners (children) crowd the starting line (the first day of first grade) that not everyone can actually begin the race in the same position at the same time. Some runners cannot make it to the end of this race and drop out before they reach the finish line (high school graduation). After completing this race, some runners decide to immediately launch themselves into another race (college), but others choose not to or simply cannot. This is no ordinary race, however, and the stakes are very, very high for all the runners.

To extend this racing metaphor even further, we can think about how the pack of runners that begins a marathon eventually fans out, with the tight clump of runners at the beginning ultimately spreading out over miles. With each passing mile, initially small differences between runners grow and grow to the point that finishing times are separated by many minutes, even hours, and, in this almost inevitable situation, those who start out the best usually finish far out in the lead.

So, let's pull this metaphor back down to the subject of this book. If differences in the *initial* level of learning in elementary school represent inequality at the starting gate, then differences in *gains* in learning in subsequent years of elementary school represent the eventual spread in the field between the starting gate and the finish line. Already in this chapter I have documented that children from Mexican immigrant families started elementary school scoring as many as 10 points lower than their native peers from other populations on math achievement tests. I then put forward various developmental domains and contexts that helped to explain this low relative performance. In other words, children from Mexican immigrant families experienced inequality at the starting gate of the elementary school. Their starting line was pushed back several yards from the one at which their peers lined up to run, and so they will be forced to play catch-up and, ultimately, have more distance to cover in the race. This is precisely how inequality is compounded over time.

Whether and how children from Mexican immigrant families fare after the start of the race is the focus of the rest of this chapter. Can they make up this distance, can they run fast enough to catch up with the other runners? To do so, they have to learn at *higher* rates than their peers in the years following the transition to elementary school. That is the only way to make up ground and time. If they learn at rates equal to their peers, they will finish the race in the same place they started, yards behind the other runners. Thus, being as good as others is not good enough. If they learn at lower rates, then they will finish the race even farther behind the other runners than they started. If so, then their inequitable start will have cumulated.

After establishing the relative positions of child populations at the starting gate, I now seek to establish what is leftover—the relative rates in learning in subsequent years that reduce, maintain, or increase these initial differences. The format of this investigation is the same as the last. The first step is to examine whether, and how much, children from Mexican immigrant families differ from their peers in *gains* in math learning *between* first grade and third grade; the second step is to determine whether the various developmental domains and contexts contribute to corresponding differences in these learning gains independently of each other; and the final step is to assess the relative contributions of these various developmental domains and contexts to these learning gains.

All the children in the ECLS-K repeated the math tests during the spring semester of third grade. Again, I calculated the average score on this test in the Mexican immigrant population and in the native White, African-American, Asian-American, and other Latino/a populations, adjusting for differences between populations in important demographic factors (e.g., sex, age) and in residential status (e.g., urbanicity, region of the country). I also added one other, important adjustment—I took into account the level of math learning in first grade. Thus the predicted math scores presented in Table 5.2 (drawn from the comparisons presented in full in Appendix Table A14) represent the test scores of children from the five populations assuming that they earned the exact same score on the test in the first grade.

Recall that, on the first-grade test, children from Mexican immigrant families scored nearly 10 points lower than native White and Asian-American children. According to Table 5.2, they also scored more than 3 points lower on the third-grade test than White and Asian-American children with whom they had demonstrated comparable levels of math learning two years earlier. In other words, they lost an additional 3 points in a few years.

Also recall that children from Mexican immigrant families scored about 3 points lower on the math test than native Latino/a children in first grade. Even taking this different starting point into account, they scored about another 3 points lower than their other Latino/a peers in third grade. Again, these points represent lost ground.

Table 5.2 Predicted Math Scores and Math Score Differentials Between First and Third Grade for Children from Various Racial/Ethnic and Immigrant Populations

Population	Predicted Score[a]	Point Differential vs. Mexican Immigrant
Children from Mexican immigrant families	92.53	–
Children from native White families	95.87	−3.34
Children from native African-American families	91.51	1.02
Children from native Asian-American families	96.16	−3.63
Children from native Latino/a families	95.01	−2.48

[a] Controlling only for sex, age, region, urbanicity, and first-grade math score.

Finally, recall that children from Mexican immigrant families scored slightly (but not in a statistically significant sense) lower than native African-American children in first grade. According to Table 5.2, they actually scored about 1 point higher than their African-American peers in third grade, although the actual comparisons that produced the numbers in Table 5.2 indicated that this differences was not statistically significant. Thus children from Mexican immigrant families did not lose or gain ground to their native African-American peers despite their different starting points.

Considering Learning Gains in Relation to Family Socioeconomic Characteristics

With these differences at first glance as the reference point for all subsequent comparisons, I set about adding, sequentially, family socioeconomic circumstances, health, psychosocial development, cognitive skills, early child care arrangements, home environment, and school enrollment to the consideration of gains in math learning between first and third grade. The first bar in each of the four comparisons in Figures 5.3 and 5.4 represents the differences at first glance. The next seven bars represent the point differentials calculated after taking each of the family socioeconomic circumstances, three developmental domains, and three developmental contexts, respectively, into account. Again, bars falling down from the center line represent point differentials in favor of the native racial or ethnic comparison population, and bars rising up from the center line represent point differentials in favor of children from Mexican immigrant families.

The differences in learning between first and third grade related to immigration from Mexico were partly a function of differences between Mexican-origin children and their native peers in the socioeconomic circumstances of

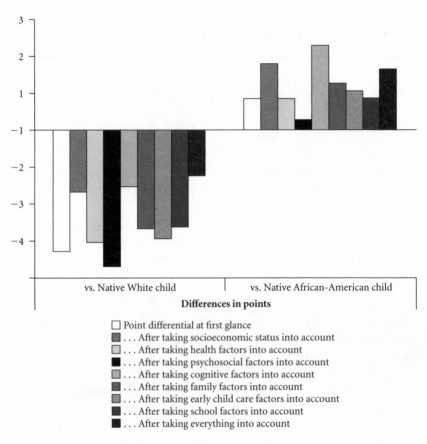

vs. Native White child | vs. Native African-American child

Differences in points

☐ Point differential at first glance
■ . . . After taking socioeconomic status into account
☐ . . . After taking health factors into account
■ . . . After taking psychosocial factors into account
▨ . . . After taking cognitive factors into account
■ . . . After taking family factors into account
▨ . . . After taking early child care factors into account
■ . . . After taking school factors into account
■ . . . After taking everything into account

Figure 5.3 Predicted point differentials in two-year gains in math test score for average child from Mexican immigrant family

their families (second bar in each comparison). Indeed, math test point differentials between Mexican immigrant families and their native White, Asian-American, and other Latino/a children were nearly 50 percent smaller than the differences at first glance when families were compared only to other families of similar socioeconomic circumstances (also see Model 2 in Table A14 in the Appendix). The differences seen at first glance did not go away, but they were much smaller. Moreover, when comparisons were made between families of similar socioeconomic circumstances, the difference in learning gains seen at first glance between children from Mexican immigrant families and their African-American peers (favoring the Mexican-origin children) actually doubled.

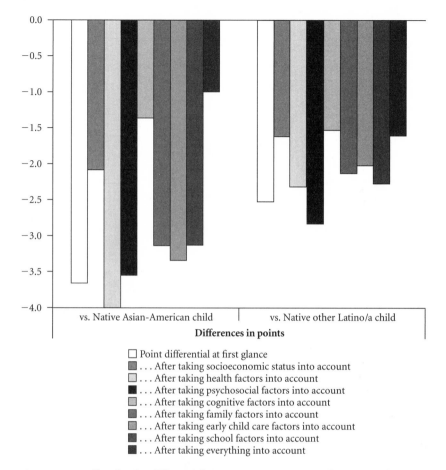

Figure 5.4 Predicted point differentials in two-year gains in math test score for average child from Mexican immigrant family

In sum, children from Mexican immigrant families had lower levels of math learning than their native White, Asian-American, and other Latino/a peers in first grade, and these differences widened somewhat over the early years of elementary school. This trend applied, albeit in reduced form, even when considering children from similar family backgrounds. On the other hand, children from Mexican immigrant families and native African-American children demonstrated remarkably similar levels of math learning, both at the onset and over time, in general, but, once the more socioeconomically disadvantaged circumstances of Mexican immigrant families were taken into account, children in these families actually fared better.

Considering Learning Gains in Relation
to Developmental Domains and Contexts

Obviously, population-level differences in socioeconomic resources play a major role in population-level differences in learning gains in the early years of elementary school. Might the various domains and contexts of child development work in the same way? I attempted to answer this question by looking at the change in point differentials on the third-grade math test associated with each of the developmental domains and contexts. Again, each domain and context was first examined separately from all others, and, again, the reference for each of these comparisons is the point differential at first glance—the point differentials observed when only sex, age, region, and urbanicity were taken into account.

Considering physical and mental health together reduced the point differential in third grade between children from Mexican immigrant families and native White children by about one-fourth of a point, compared to the differences at first glance. This consideration did not alter the point differential between children from Mexican immigrant families and native African-American children, and it increased the point differential between children from Mexican immigrant families and native Asian-American and native other Latino/a children by about one-fourth of a point. When physical health but not mental health was taken into account, the point differential between children from Mexican immigrant families and White children was reduced by about one point, and the point differential between children from Mexican immigrant families and Asian-American and other Latino/a children was reduced by about one-fourth of a point. On the other hand, when mental health but not physical health was taken into account, I saw only small changes in the differentials seen at first glance.

As for the other domains of development, taking the two psychosocial factors (on which children from Mexican immigrant families rated fairly well) into account increased the point differentials between children from Mexican immigrant families and their native White and other Latino/a peers by about half a point. Taking the two cognitive skills (on which children from Mexican immigrant families rated fairly poorly) into account reduced the point differentials between children from Mexican immigrant families and their native White, Asian-American, and other Latino/a peers by between 1.5 and 2 points and doubled the point differential between children from Mexican immigrant families and native African-American children.

Turning to the contexts of child development, immigration-related differences in math gains between first and third grade did fluctuate according to corresponding differences in families, child care arrangements, and schools. In order of importance, the point differentials between children from Mexican immigrant families and their native White, Asian-American, and other Latino/a peers decreased by about two-thirds of a point after adjusting for differences in family learning activities, half a point after adjusting for differences in school environments, and one-third of a point after adjusting for differences in early child care (all relative to the differences at first glance). These contexts did not greatly alter the differentials between children from Mexican immigrant families and their native African-American peers, with the exception of the family context. Taking into account differences in family contexts between these two populations increased the initial differential by half a point in favor of children from Mexican immigrant families.

Considering Learning Gains in Relation to Everything

The final piece of this analysis is the consideration of what the relative positioning of the five racial or ethnic populations on the third-grade math test would be if they all looked the same in terms of their family socioeconomic circumstances and their domains and contexts of development. The final bar in Figures 5.3 and 5.4 captures these point differentials derived from the comprehensive treatment of third-grade math learning (see Table A15 in the Appendix for the full results of this comprehensive treatment).

Before discussing the racial/ethnic and immigration-related differences in gains in learning between first and third grade, let me first describe which of the developmental factors contributed to these gains and how much they contributed. Of the socioeconomic characteristics and the various aspects of developmental domains and contexts, five were associated with greater gains in math learning during this time span: family socioeconomic status, self-regulation, home learning activities, parental involvement in education, and preschool math skills. Five were associated with lower gains: poor physical health, internalizing symptoms, social competence, racially segregated schools, and high rates of school poverty. In terms of the magnitude of these associations, the factors just mentioned fell into four categories, from largest to smallest in magnitude:

1. Preschool cognitive skills.
2. Self-regulation.

3. The two school factors, social competence, and family socioeconomic status.

4. The two health factors and the two family factors.

Shifting the focus from gains in learning back to racial/ethnic and immigration-related differences in these gains, children from Mexican immigrant families scored between 1 point and 1.5 points lower on the third-grade math test than their native White and other Latino/a peers who were similar to them on family socioeconomic circumstances and on the various developmental domains and contexts. Once all these other factors were taken into account, they demonstrated essentially the same level of gains in math learning between first and third grade as their native Asian-American peers, and they outgained their native African-American peers by nearly 2 points.

Math Learning Gains Summary

One aspect of inequality is the baseline level of difference, or inequality at the starting gate. Another is change in inequality over time. The focus of this half of the chapter was on inequality over time—identifying instances of both lost and gained ground in math learning between first and third grade.

First, children from Mexican immigrant families lost ground compared to their native White, Asian-American, and other Latino/a peers. Improving the socioeconomic circumstances of Mexican immigrant families would eliminate a good chunk of these differences, and boosting the cognitive skills with which these children start elementary school would also stanch the losing of ground among children from these families in the early years of elementary school. Cultivating more learning activities in Mexican immigrant families and improving the physical health and school environments of the children in these families would make a smaller but important dent in these differences in learning. Clearly, the psychosocial skills of children from Mexican immigrant families are one of their great resources, to the point that the extent of lost ground would have been greater if they were not so developed in these psychological terms.

Second, children from Mexican immigrant families did not lose any ground, on average, to native African-American children during this same time span. Yet this general picture transformed into something quite different when considered from other angles. Chipping away at the disadvantages faced by children from Mexican immigrant families in their family circumstances and in their general development would actually lead to gained ground for children from Mexican immigrant families.

Whether considering gained or lost ground, however, the contribution of child development and developmental contexts to learning differences between racial or ethnic populations was far smaller three years into elementary school than at the beginning of school. In other words, differences between children from Mexican immigrant families may not have grown over these years, but they did not shrink either. Instead, they stabilized into parallel trajectories that, because of differences in starting points, remained unequal.

6 What Have We Learned?

BY THIS POINT, I have thrown out quite a torrent of information, and all the numbers—including how I arrived at these numbers and what they mean—are probably a bit overwhelming. Given this potential for overload, stepping back to recap and then organize all that has been revealed in the preceding chapters is probably a smart move on my part.

Entering Elementary School

The theoretical model underlying this study—its basic blueprint if you will—posited that some important developmental experiences in the burgeoning population of children from Mexican immigrant families placed these children at risk, relative to their peers, for lower rates of learning in math during the early years of elementary school. The first step in determining whether this *theory* adequately captured *reality* was to compare children from Mexican immigrant families to their native peers from other major racial or ethnic populations on different domains and contexts of child development.

Children from Mexican immigrant families did differ systematically from their peers in various aspects of child development in the years leading up to the transition into elementary school. In one domain of development and in two contexts of development, they appeared to be at a general disadvantage. Compared to other children, including other minority children, Mexican-origin children entered elementary school with less developed cognitive skills, at least in terms of early math knowledge and English proficiency, and with less experience in important learning activities at home. Moreover, the elementary schools that they entered were highly disadvantaged in many ways compared to the schools serving their peers. In other words, they brought less preparation for academic coursework with them when they entered schools less prepared to serve them effectively.

In only one domain of development could children from Mexican immigrant families be considered to have a general advantage over their peers at the start of elementary school. These children fared fairly well on aspects of psychosocial development, especially their ability to self-regulate their behavior in school. Thus, despite other riskier aspects of their lives and their living situations, children from Mexican immigrant families were emotionally equipped for the rigors of early education—they were school ready (or, readier) in this sense.

One domain of child development and one context of child development offered something of a mixed bag for children from Mexican immigrant families in terms of advantages and disadvantages in the early learning process. Beginning with health, children from Mexican immigrant families entered elementary school with generally poorer physical health but generally better mental health than their peers. As for early child care, these children were less likely to transition into elementary school from preschool programs than their peers, but they were the most likely of all children to be cared for solely by parents in the years leading up to elementary school.

The summary that I have laid out here does require a few qualifying comments. First, Mexican immigrant families are highly disadvantaged in socioeconomic terms, with low rates of educational attainment and earnings among parents, and, obviously, these socioeconomic disadvantages can affect how children develop, how their families operate, and what social contexts they traverse. Consequently, ignoring the potential for socioeconomic circumstances to drive all the differences, especially the apparent risks, laid out so far would not be fair to Mexican immigrant families or to the children in these families. Yes, taking into account differences in parents' education, income, and other elements of socioeconomic status across populations does make the situation of children from Mexican immigrant families seem more hopeful, but for the most part it does not alter the general conclusion that the life circumstances of these children potentially place them at risk for truncated trajectories of learning in elementary school and, through these early differences, for truncated trajectories of educational attainment in the long run.

Second, I have written this summary in broad brushstrokes, ignoring many of the nuances that I spelled out in earlier chapters, in order to craft a more cohesive final message. Depending on the comparison being made (e.g., versus native Whites, versus native Asian-American children), the *relative* well-being of children from Mexican immigrant families did fluctuate somewhat. What I have described here is the *general* story that emerged from all these different comparisons.

Third, the life circumstances of children from Mexican immigrant families cannot, obviously, be summed up by six developmental domains and contexts or by the limited set of factors I selected to represent these domains and contexts. Importantly, many of the factors not considered here might be areas in which children from Mexican immigrant families have clear advantages over their peers (e.g., familism, community support). If so, I have neglected some of the bright spots in this population in favor of a far less positive profile. On this point I would argue that how I chose and assessed these developmental domains and contexts was driven by established knowledge about the connection between child development and early education. In this way I was working with identified risk and protective factors in the general literature to identify targets of intervention in this specific population. Stated another way, I was looking for things to change to improve the prospects of children from Mexican immigrant families in elementary school, and the results presented in this book suggest that I found them.

Navigating Elementary School

The second step in assessing the validity of the theoretical blueprint of this book was to determine whether these selected differences in developmental domains and contexts related to emigration from Mexico translated into corresponding differences in learning in a core curriculum — math — of elementary school. In other words, children from Mexican immigrant families looked different from their peers in several important education-related circumstances of their lives, but did these differences really matter in the end?

In short, children from Mexican immigrant families had lower levels of math learning in first grade than their native White, Asian-American, and other Latino/a peers and made fewer gains in math learning between first grade and third grade than these peers, but, for the most part, their learning in math was somewhat similar to their native African-American peers. These racial/ethnic and immigration-related differences in early learning *were* related to the general developmental experiences of children from the various racial or ethnic populations and therefore might be responsive to interventions aimed at these developmental experiences.

Table 6.1 Contributions to Differences in Math Learning in First Grade Related to Emigration from Mexico

Category	Contexts or Domains
Category 1[a]	Preschool cognitive skills Family socioeconomic circumstances
Category 2[b]	Education-focused family processes Health Psychosocial skills
Category 3[c]	School context Early child care

[a] Each domain or context accounts for at least 50% of the point differentials on the first-grade math test between children from Mexican immigrant families and their White, Asian-American, and other Latino/a peers.

[b] Each domain or context accounts for roughly 25% of the point differentials.

[c] Each context accounts for roughly 10% of the point differentials.

Basically, I calculated the amount of the point differentials between children from Mexican immigrant families and their native peers on the first-grade math test attributable to racial/ethnic and immigration-related differences in the six domains and contexts of child development. These calculations were based on the independent, not comprehensive, assessments of each domain and context, and so substantial overlap exists among the amount of the differentials that I attribute to each one. The goal here is to provide something of a flow chart indicating what the academic outcome of systematic changes in each domain and context might be. As seen in Table 6.1, domains and contexts fell into three rough categories.

The first category contained the domains and contexts that accounted for more than 50 percent of the point differentials between children from Mexican immigrant families and their White, Asian-American, and other Latino/a peers on the first-grade math test. These were the *major* factors. The most important, by far, were the preschool cognitive skills. Taking them into account eliminated virtually all differences between children from Mexican immigrant families and their native peers and, more specifically, actually opened up an advantage for children from Mexican immigrant families compared to their African-American peers. Thus, if children from Mexican immigrant families came to school with the same early knowledge of math and the same English proficiency as native children, they would demonstrate rates of learning similar to, or in some cases better than, these children. I touched on the socioeconomic issue earlier, and it played out in the investigation of learning too. Put simply, roughly half the differences in math learning in first grade that we have observed here were related to the more disadvantaged socioeconomic circumstances of Mexican immigrant families. Obviously, many of these effects were channeled through the other domains and contexts, but socioeconomic circumstances and preschool cognitive skills seem to be the major origins of differences in early learning.

The second category included three domains and contexts of child development that accounted for between 25 percent and 33 percent of the point differentials in first-grade math test performance related to emigration from Mexico. If two kinds of family processes directly focused on education—home reading activities and parental involvement at school—were the same in Mexican immigrant families as in other families, then, according to my calculations, children of Mexican immigrants make up about 2 or 3 points in math learning on their native peers. The same makeup would happen if we enhanced the physical health of these children to a level comparable to their peers. On the other hand, the learning gap would grow by a similar amount if we somehow equalized the mental health (or self-regulation) of children from Mexican immigrant families and their peers because, for the most part, such an equalization would mean *reducing* the adjustment and functioning of children from Mexican immigrant families, or taking away the advantages that they had.

The third category included the two developmental contexts that accounted for less than one-quarter of the point differentials in first-grade math test performance related to emigration from Mexico. Taking into account the disadvantages that children from Mexican immigrant families exhibited in the public domain (lower enrollment in preschool, higher enrollment in racially and economically segregated schools) would knock off about 1 point of the gap between children from Mexican immigrant families and their native White, Asian-American, and other Latino/a peers. These factors, therefore, mattered; they just mattered to a much lower degree than the other aspects of child development considered here.

By expanding the focus from the start of elementary school to the first several years of elementary school, I found that these basic patterns remained, although they did shift in subtle but important ways. First, the point differentials between children from Mexican immigrant families and their native White, Asian-American, and other Latino/a peers were smaller in third grade than in first grade. Because these third-grade levels of math learning captured gains in learning between first and third grade, these smaller differences actually indicated further distancing between children from Mexican immigrant families and their native peers. In other words, the distance between the two kept grow- ing, but the rate of this growth was starting to slow down—not reverse, just slow down. Second, these differences in math learning over time were accounted for by the differences in domains and contexts of child development before school entry, although in a less pronounced way than was evident in the investigation of math learning in first grade. This finding indicates that preschool differences in development had a continuing impact on learning in elementary school, but the magnitude of this impact was weakening over time.

Child Development, Schooling, and Emigration from Mexico

Children from Mexican immigrant families have lower levels of learning in math than many of their native peers during the early years of elementary school. These early learning trends could have far-reaching and cumulative ef- fects on these children's lives as well as on the prospects of the Mexican-origin population as a whole. Fortunately, these trends are also related to things that we know a great deal about, things that we can target. Some of these things matter more than others, and some are easier to change than others. We do, however, have some levers with which we can work.

7   Where Do We Go from Here?

ON ONE SIDE IS KNOWLEDGE, on the other action. The trick is to translate the first into the second. Over the last several decades scientists interested in the topics of child development, family life, and education have tried their hands at this tricky form of translation. From *Brown v. Board of Education* to Head Start, public television, early child care, and welfare reform, psychologists, sociologists, economists, and physicians have made their mark in the world of social policy on local, state, and national levels. They achieved this by using the knowledge derived from their research to inform interventions and programs, by drawing on the scientific method to evaluate existing policies, and by actively participating in the crafting and delivery of services.

As I stated fairly clearly in the opening chapter of this book, I too aim for this common ground of science and service. My goal has been to produce a body of knowledge about the transition to elementary school of children from Mexican immigrant families that can inform social policies aimed at alleviating the educational inequalities that have long-term consequences for the socio-economic prospects of the Mexican-origin population in the United States. In that vein I use this chapter to put forward some general policy recommendations that, in my view, arise from the findings reported in this book.

An Issue Whose Time Has Come

As I explained in Chapter 6, the long and short of this book is this: Children from Mexican immigrant families are forced to play catch-up from the get-go. To borrow a phrase from Valerie Lee and David Burkham, what they face is inequality at the starting gate. Of course, we know from decades of scientific research and even from casual observation that the U.S. educational system is not well equipped to help children from Mexican immigrant families, or children in any disadvantaged population, close this early inequality. If anything, the system makes it worse.

This general pattern suggests something ominous: a deepening of inequality in our society as the Mexican immigrant population expands and more and more of the future citizens of the United States lose their educational opportunities. This deepening inequality is, of course, a problem for Mexican immigrants and their families and communities, but it is also a problem for everyone else in the United States. American society will be damaged economically by a growing pool of workers who lack appropriate education and training for many sectors of the labor force and by an expanding burden on social programs. It will be damaged politically by a burgeoning portion of the population and electorate cut out of the decision-making process, essentially disenfranchised, and, if history has shown us anything, ultimately alienated. It will be damaged socially by the yawning chasm between haves and have-nots, between white, black, and brown, and by the increasing segregation of how we live and work. It will be damaged culturally by the extreme counterevidence to our proud historical claims to be a free, just, and equitable society. For those middle-class and upper-class citizens of the United States who do not buy such "damage," perhaps their self-interest will be awakened by the realization that today's children of Mexican immigrants will go a long way toward determining the liquidity of our retirement, Social Security, and pensions systems tomorrow.[1] In other words, how Mexican immigrants, and their children, are welcomed into American society and how well American society eases and assists this transition will go a long way to determining the future of the American people—all of them.

Mexican immigration and the inequalities that surround it, therefore, are issues of national importance. As such, they require thoughtful action. I would suggest, based on what I have found in the course of this study, that two ways to put some thought into our actions would be to start early and to expand our view of what education is and what it entails. Let me be more specific. First, inequality, as with so many other things in life, grows, develops, and solidifies over time. It is the proverbial weed in the garden. If we wait too long to do something about it, the roots are too entrenched and our efforts to eradicate it are ultimately futile. If we strike early, we can yank the weed out by the roots completely so that it does not become a problem again. Second, in thinking about education, we have to consider what children do, how they feel, where they live their lives—so much more than their IQs—to understand how children do in school. Moreover, we have to consider population-level differences in these things to understand inequalities in education. Bringing these two themes together, what we need to do in terms of demographic inequality is target the educational inequality that underlies it, and what we need to do in terms of educational inequality is target the earliest years of school and consider how *life* seeps into the school.

Addressing Inequality

Many different approaches can be taken to informing social policy that targets the inequalities related to emigration from Mexico, and this one is mine. I have developed a sort of symbolic algebra: What might happen to Y if we make a change to X? In this case, Y is early educational inequalities between children from Mexican immigrant families and their peers, and X is an amalgam of factors tapping the various aspects of the general development of children and the settings in which this general development takes place. What does this algebra tell us?

First, these are *some* of the major risks to children from Mexican immigrant families as they start their school careers in first grade: lower level of entry-level cognitive skills *valued* by U.S. schools, fewer socioeconomic resources in the family, lower rates of parent-child activities at home *valued* by U.S. schools, poorer physical health, lower rates of preschool enrollment, and school segregation. Fortunately, these are things that we can do something about if we try. This is certainly not easy, and it takes a long time, many resources, and a great deal of manpower. It can, however, be done.

In fact, many tools are already in place to alleviate some of these risks. Public transfer programs target socioeconomic disadvantage and poverty, public insurance programs and community clinics target health, programs such as Head Start target early education, and educational reform targets low-performing schools and school segregation across the country. Many of these tools have significant problems in planning and implementation, and few of them specifically focus on the Mexican immigrant population. My point in bringing them up is not that they are cure-alls, for certainly they have not yet proven to be so for any population, but that they are a good start, a good foundation on which to build. With these programs we have established channels of service from the public or private sector to populations in need. Now we need to dedicate the time and energy to make sure that they actually work.

Second, these are *some* of the resources that children from Mexican immigrant families bring with them when they enter the U.S. educational system: good mental health, self-regulating abilities, and high levels of social competence. That all these resources are so personal in nature suggests that children from Mexican immigrant families are internally quite strong, most likely because of the tight-knit nature of their families and communities, and that they and their parents are up to the challenges before them. These are not things that need to be changed; they are strengths that will facilitate outside efforts to serve children from Mexican immigrant families. Perhaps this picture of the strong and competent Mexican immigrant child suggests, most of all, that we—meaning the larger American society—need to invest more of *our* resources in these children so that *their* resources can win out in the end.

Whole-Child Perspective as an Orienting Philosophy of Service

That, by far, the most important categories of factors contributing to the early learning of children from Mexican immigrant families were entry-level cognitive skills and family socioeconomic circumstances speaks to the difficulty of crafting social policy to reduce inequality related to emigration from Mexico. Yet the significance of these two sets of factors also points to the need for more holistic perspectives on children's lives, for the need to focus on how pieces of the puzzle fit together.

Family socioeconomic status is important to early educational trajectories, and the lower socioeconomic status of Mexican immigrant families certainly seems to explain a lot of the lower math learning of children in these families in the early years of elementary school. This leads to a simple conclusion: Let's raise the socioeconomic status of Mexican immigrant families. That is the ideal solution, of course, but one must wonder whether it is the most realistic solution. The truth is that the United States has never really developed a large-scale method of improving the socioeconomic status of disadvantaged families in the short run, although other countries have been more successful in doing so. At the same time, improving the socioeconomic circumstances of the poor, although popular in theory, has not proven to be politically expedient. In other words, it is a hot-button issue in a society that has often demonized welfare and related programs. If targeting socioeconomic status is as difficult as socioeconomic circumstances are crucial to educational inequality, then what can we do? Our best bet is to focus on the more proximate mediators of socioeconomic effects on early education—in other words, the immediate aspects of children's lives that explain why socioeconomic status influences early educational experiences. We have to ask the question of *why* socioeconomic status matters and then target our answers.

Some major reasons that socioeconomic status plays an important role in early education are the same factors that I have considered in this study. Socioeconomic status is a cause of low English language proficiency, poor health, and bad schools. Thus, improving language services, providing better health care, and reorganizing schools—really doing these things, not just halfheartedly—may blunt some of the effects of socioeconomic status on early learning. Given that socioeconomic status is such a major contributor to educational inequalities related to emigration from Mexico, these coordinated efforts could raise the relative level of school readiness of children from Mexican immigrant families. Importantly, *very* importantly, raising the school readiness of these children would likely translate into more positive educational trajectories in primary and secondary school, which would facilitate college matriculation, which would improve socioeconomic prospects for these children as adults. In the end, targeting the start of elementary school in such a holistic way could be an effective long-term method of achieving the goal of improving the socioeconomic circumstances of families, the same goal that has been so difficult and unpopular in the short term.

The cognitive skills that children bring with them when they start school, including their already existing knowledge about key school subjects, are absolutely crucial to how well they do in school. Children do not always enter school with the same baseline even if they are equal in actual intelligence, and, unfortunately, differences in baseline too often correspond to demographic demarcations. These early disparities send different child populations onto different tracks. Again, however, the answers to this particular problematic component of the school transition model can be found in other components of the model. How do we raise the language proficiency of children from Mexican immigrant families *before* they start school? How do we get them exposed to math *before* they enter an actual math class?

To me, the best way to do this is by expanding access to preschool education and by promoting certain learning activities in Mexican immigrant families. For example, the Foundation for Child Development in New York is part of an organized effort to create an aligned PK-3 (prekindergarten through third grade) system of education, which would allow many groups, such as Mexican immigrant children, to catch up with more advantaged groups before the start of formal schooling. As a universal, such a program would go far beyond the narrower reach of Head Start, which has had some positive effects on school readiness. That the child care factor in my study was relatively weak compared to other components of the school transition model probably speaks to the great diversity in the quality of preschool programs among children in the ECLS-K sample, a diversity that can water down the apparent benefits of such programs. As evidenced by the findings of the NICHD Early Child Care Research Network,[2] quality of care is more important than type of care, but the ECLS-K allowed the consideration of only the type of care. This issue, however, actually adds to the calls for an aligned, organized, developmentally appropriate approach to early education. As another example, schools can do a great deal to involve parents in learning activities when children actually enter school by offering reading programs and learning supplies (e.g., books, especially Spanish-language books), and, as the wealth of research on Catholic schools has shown, common curricula for all students within schools can go a long way toward quickly eliminating even sizable gaps in school readiness between child populations that exist on the first day of school.

Taking the major factors that put children from Mexican immigrant families at academic risk at the start of their elementary school careers and then working backward through the other aspects of child development related to these major risk factors is, in my opinion, a potentially rewarding strategy. This strategy, and others like it that are rooted in the whole-child philosophy, can provide leverage in the age-old conundrum about utilizing social policy to alter societal inequalities, specifically, the need to balance relevance and doability. What I have laid out just now is a suggestion to use doable means (e.g., actionable aspects of child development) as an end run around the most relevant means of improving the early educational prospects of children from Mexican immigrant families (e.g., socioeconomic status). The growing movement toward school-linked services—in which both the mission and the physical institution of schools are expanded to include services for parents and noneducational services for children[3]—fits into this philosophy. Imagine an elementary school that included preschool programs for future students and resource centers for the parents of these future students, that included real health care services for students and parents, and that included language tutoring for young and old, and then imagine how Mexican immigrant parents and their children would benefit from living in a community with a school like that.

Some Caveats to the Discussion of Policy

As I explained in Chapter 1, national-level demographic analyses play a vital role in policy-focused research because they give the best sense of the potential

universality of important trends and the potential consequences of policy action. Yet these analyses, including mine, also have some limitations that must
be met and answered by other types of research. For example, national-level
survey data do not provide the best means of establishing causality. In other
words, my study has demonstrated that health is related to the early education
of children from Mexican immigrant families, but some sort of experimental
design would do the best job of ascertaining whether bad health *causes* educational problems. As another example, my study focuses on the entire population of children from Mexican immigrant families, assessing how they look as
a single group, and that ignores much of the variability and diversity in this
population. Qualitative approaches (such as interviews with and observations
of families) more effectively bring out the individual voices within this population. Thus my study has set up a basic plan for policy action that points to
certain potential leverage points. As such, it will work best when partnered with
other studies that delve into some of its nuances, establish some of its facts,
and evaluate its suggestions in pilot programs. Only in this way can scientific
research take its much needed place in the policy world.

Obviously, this line of research has many sequels—expanding the list of
developmental factors considered, examining other areas of learning and academic achievement, investigating whether changes in developmental domains
and contexts after the start of elementary school add to the significance of
preschool domains and contexts, following the trajectories of children as they
move through the remainder of elementary school and beyond. All these elabo-
rations are needed. The more we know about this population, the better.

The decisions that I have made in setting up this study may also be ques-
tioned by others. First, why did I set first grade as the start of elementary school
and not kindergarten? Although kindergarten is technically a part of the elementary school system, it is not mandatory, does not usually follow a structured curriculum of coursework, and may be part-time or part-year. First grade,
although often the second year in school, is the first year of formal schooling
for most children.

Second, why focus on child development as a component of educational
inequality rather than more structural and systemic forces? After all, the differences in developmental domains and contexts related to emigration from
Mexico that I have outlined in this book are, without a doubt, shaped by much
larger social forces, such as segregation, discrimination, and the politics of divi-
sion. What I have done here is target the end points of these larger social forces,

where they have the most immediate impact on children's lives. In other words, given that health is one channel through which a long history of social and economic hardship has jeopardized the early education of children from Mexican immigrant families, can attempts to improve the health of these children blunt some of the extremely negative consequences of these larger social forces so many years in the making? Given that another channel has been the complete public disregard for the schools that children from Mexican immigrant families attend, can efforts to send these children to new schools or to improve their current schools help to stanch the generational transfer of disadvantage? Here, I take a pointedly focused approach to the lives of children from Mexican immigrant families in which I consider what changes to certain aspects of their lives and environments might help us in our attempts to educate these children.

Third, why did I select the particular aspects of the developmental domains and contexts that I considered in this study? As I have mentioned in previous chapters, the aspects that I chose to consider often weighted the scales against children from Mexican immigrant families. For example, I focused on cognitive skills that children from Mexican immigrant families would be less likely to have and ignored areas of cognition in which they would be more likely to have an advantage (e.g., cognitive flexibility cultivated by true bilingualism). My general intent was to consider aspects of child development and parenting *known* to be valued by U.S. schools. In many cases what was valued by U.S. schools disadvantaged children from Mexican immigrant families, which is an important reality of emigration from Mexico until these value systems change.

If policy is to be adequately informed in the United States, then it should be based on a sound body of scientific evidence—an accumulation of evidence from different researchers working with different models and different analytical tools and making different decisions about different issues. Collective knowledge is the ultimate goal. This study—and all the decisions that I made to bring it to completion—is one step in this larger collective enterprise. Who wants to join me?

Epilogue

THE HISTORY OF MEXICAN IMMIGRATION to the United States has been fraught with conflict (the uproar in early 2006 over congressional attempts to reform immigration laws is a particularly striking example), and so has the history of scientific research on this important immigration flow. For decades educational researchers in the United States treated immigrants from Mexico as a threat to U.S. schools and blamed the lower rate of educational success among Mexican-American children on the children themselves and on their parents. This *deficit* model of educational research clearly created many hard feelings, clouded our understanding of the complex issues surrounding the education of this growing population, and hamstrung any attempts to effectively serve the children and families in this population.

Clearly, we have to move forward. We have to move forward to promote educational attainment in the population of Mexican immigrants in the United States, not because the growth of this population is a *threat* but because it is a potential *resource*. We have to move forward to ensure that this concept that we have so long called the American dream is an actual, achievable goal and not just an ideology. As William Julius Wilson has argued about research on the African-American experience, the first step in moving past hard feelings to capture a true and usable understanding of African-American families and communities is to throw out the deficit model and then bridge the insights from perspectives that focus on individual behavior and those that focus on systemic forces. I argue that this book on Mexican immigrants is in that same spirit.

Emigration from Mexico is a powerful force in the twenty-first century, and if the demographic forecasts of the U.S. census are to be believed, this power will only increase in the coming years. The long-term consequences of this power are still unknown and unformed. To maximize the possibility that these consequences will be positive, we have to recognize that the insidious, pernicious nature of inequality has affected Mexican immigrants and their families, determine how this big picture of inequality plays out in the small picture of children's and parents' lives, and then figure out how the small picture can be used to alter the big picture and vice versa. Targeting specific aspects of the lives of children from Mexican immigrant families and of the places where they live their lives is one way to do so *if* this approach can then promote individual educational trajectories that over time and collectively promote the socioeconomic circumstances of the Mexican-origin population. One day, perhaps, such entrenched inequality will disappear in the face of such success.

As Archimedes famously declared, a simple fulcrum is all that is needed to move the world. The quest to ensure that the American dream is no longer kept from Mexican immigrants is, in its essence, a search for a fulcrum. I would think that this is an enterprise of which we would all like to be part.

Appendix

Appendix

Description of the ECLS-K Data

The National Center for Education Statistics (NCES) at the U.S. Department of Education constructed the Early Childhood Longitudinal Study—Kindergarten Cohort (ECLS-K), which began as a nationally representative sample of U.S. kindergartners in the fall of 1998, in order to allow the in-depth investigation of educational processes and inequalities at the beginning of formal schooling and across the early years of schooling. Detailed descriptions of the ECLS-K sample design and data collection can be found in comprehensive research reports by Denton and West[1] and Lee and Burkham[2] as well as on the ECLS-K website.[3]

The ECLS-K sampling frame was split into three separate but nested stages. First, the NCES randomly selected approximately 100 primary sampling units, with the most common sampling unit being an official U.S. county. Second, within these primary sampling units, the NCES randomly sampled approximately 1,000 schools that contained a kindergarten, with public and private schools selected from separate sampling frames. Third, an average of about 23 children per school were then randomly sampled within these schools. Once the 22,782 children for the sample were identified and recruited, data collection proceeded at various stages. The first data collection occurred in the fall of 1998, which corresponded to the first few months of kindergarten. Children were given diagnostic tests in several arenas of cognitive achievement (e.g., oral language skills, reading skills, math knowledge). For the overwhelming majority of these children, one parent participated in an in-depth interview over the phone or at home in the language of his or her choice, and one school administrator (typically a principal) and one teacher filled out a paper and pencil survey. Attempts were then made to repeat this same procedure several months later in the final part of kindergarten during the spring of 1999. A small portion of the original sample dropped out of the study between these two points.

After the completion of the 1998–99 school year, data collections were repeated at somewhat regular intervals. The data collection in the fall semester of first grade (1999) targeted only a special subsample of children (25%). This data collection was designed for research on specific topics (e.g., summer learning losses) and is not generally included in most analyses of the ECLS-K data. Regular data collection resumed in the spring semester of first grade (2000), when the full sample, minus dropouts, again engaged in the full battery of interviews, assessments, and surveys. The final two data collections occurred in the spring semester of third grade (2002) and in the spring semester of fifth grade (2004). With some modifications and additions, these collections essentially replicated the same design as the kindergarten data collection. At each stage some children and families dropped out of the study. Approximately three-fourths, however, maintained their participation throughout each stage.

My particular study focused on a subset of the full ECLS-K sample. Specifically, I used a set of three selection filters, each one demanded by the aims of the study. First, to create clean, accessible comparison categories against which to assess the children of Mexican immigrant families, I narrowed the sample to children from the four largest racial or ethnic populations in the United States: non-Latino/a White, non-Latino/a African-American, Asian-American, and Latino/a (which included all Mexican-origin children). Second, because of the need to track the basic experiences and learning trajectories of children from Mexican immigrant families over several years of schooling, I selected only those children who participated in data collection in both stages of kindergarten, the spring semester of first grade, and the spring semester of third grade. This longitudinal selection filter excluded the largest number of cases. Third, because most predictors were generated from parent and teacher reports, I selected only the children who had a parent and teacher interviewed in kindergarten.

Table A1 presents the demographic breakdown from each stage of this sample selection process. Cumulatively, application of the selection filters biased the sample somewhat toward social advantage (e.g., slightly higher socioeconomic status, more two-parent families). This bias is certainly not ideal, but it is a natural by-product of large-scale longitudinal data collection. Moreover, each selection filter was absolutely necessary to effectively conduct this line

Table A1 Characteristics for Each Stage of the Sample Selection Process

Characteristic	Mean (SD)		
	Sample 1[a]	Sample 2[b]	Sample 3[c]
Sex (female)	0.49 (0.50)	0.49 (0.50)	0.50 (0.50)
Age (years)	6.23 (0.37)	6.23 (0.37)	6.22 (0.37)
White	0.60 (0.49)	0.59 (0.49)	0.60 (0.49)
Socioeconomic status	0.03 (0.80)	0.05 (0.80)	0.05 (0.80)
Family structure (two-parent)	0.64 (0.48)	0.69 (0.46)	0.70 (0.46)
N	18,890	14,021	13,003

[a] All White, African-American, Asian-American, and Latino/a children who participated in the first wave of data collection during the fall semester of kindergarten.

[b] Sample 1, excluding children who did not participate during the spring semester of first grade or the spring semester of third grade.

[c] Sample 2, excluding children who did not have a parent or teacher interviewed in kindergarten.

of research. This slight bias must be remembered in the interpretation of all analyses performed on this ECLS-K subsample.

Description of the ECLS-K Measures

Focal Measures

In the basic set-up of the study presented in Chapter 2, I briefly summarize the measurement of three sets of factors that are the central focus of this book: race or ethnicity and immigrant status, family socioeconomic characteristics, and math learning. I take the time and space now to describe these measures, plus the basic control variables used in each stage of data analysis in full.

Race or Ethnicity and Immigrant Status   The NCES created a composite scale of race and ethnicity based on the reports of parents in the fall semester of kindergarten and on other information. This scale included eight categories, which I then reorganized and collapsed into four main categories representing the largest racial or ethnic populations in the United States according to the U.S. Census Bureau[4]: non-Latino/a White, non-Latino/a African-American, Asian-American, and Latino/a. This focus eliminated a small number of children not in these populations (e.g., Native American children). Next, I pulled out a subset of the Latino/a population on the basis of parents' reports of the birthplace of their children in the fall semester of kindergarten and of themselves in the spring semester of first grade. Specifically, all children who were born in Mexico (the first generation) or who were born in the United States to at least one Mexican-born parent (the second generation) were separated from the larger Latino/a category, grouped together, and labeled children from Mexican immigrant families.

This coding scheme resulted in five mutually exclusive dummy variables: children from Mexican immigrant families ($n = 769$) and then White ($n = 7{,}748$), African-American ($n = 1{,}802$), Asian-American ($n = 1{,}586$), and other Latino/a children ($n = 1{,}093$). Of special note are three issues related to this coding scheme. First, the ECLS-K did not allow the identification of the third generation and higher generation in any population, meaning that a U.S.-born child with U.S.-born parents and Mexican-born grandparents (or great-grandparents, etc.) could not be differentiated from other Latino/a children. Thus the other Latino/a category includes some children with Mexican roots as well as all other children, regardless of generation, with roots in Latin America. Second, some children in the four non-Mexican categories could have been first- or second-generation immigrants, especially Asian-American and other Latino/a children. To take this internal heterogeneity into account when comparing children from Mexican immigrant families to children from these other populations, I created a binary marker of non-Mexican immigrant status (where 1 = foreign-born child or U.S.-born child with foreign-born parents in the White, African-American, Asian-American, or other Latino/a population), which was then used as a control in all analyses.

Family Socioeconomic Characteristics   The first measure in the set of socioeconomic factors was, fittingly, family socioeconomic status, a measure constructed by the NCES. In the fall semester of kindergarten, parents reported the level of educational attainment of both mothers or female guardians and fathers or male guardians (1 = eighth grade or below; 2 = ninth to twelfth grade; 3 = high school graduation or equivalent; 4 = vocational or technical program; 5 = some college; 6 = bachelor's degree; 7 = some graduate or professional training; 8 = master's degree; 9 = doctorate or professional degree), the annual income earned by the family (all money, in dollars, earned by all household members in the last year), and the occupations of mothers or female guardians and fathers or male guardians (which the NCES grouped into 22 categories and then assigned occupational prestige scores established for the General Social Survey). The NCES standardized these items so that they were on the same scale (mean = 0; standard deviation = 1) and then averaged them for each family to create the final scale. To impute missing data for families missing on any one of the constituent items in the scale, the NCES used a hotdeck strategy, in which any respondent missing data on a particular item was given the value of another respondent randomly selected from a group who demonstrated many similarities with the missing respondent on other survey items. More information on the construction of this scale by the NCES, including the hotdeck imputation strategy, is available in the ECLS-K codebooks and is also explained by Denton and West.[5]

Closely related to family socioeconomic status is federal poverty status; indeed, federal poverty status is partly embedded in family socioeconomic status. I first divided parents' self-reported household income by their self-reported household size to measure per capita income within each family. I then compared this per capita income to the federal poverty line established by the U.S. government for 1998 (which was $16,450 for a family of four) to create a binary marker that differentiated those families who fell at or below the poverty threshold for the first year of data collection from all other families in the sample.

In the fall semester of kindergarten, parents also filled out a household roster, in which they listed all people currently living in the household with the child. The NCES collapsed these rosters into a more accessible scale that included nine categories (1 = biological mother and father; 2 = biological mother and other father; 3 = other mother and biological father; 4 = biological mother only; 5 = biological father only; 6 = two adopted parents; 7 = one adopted parent; 8 = related guardians; 9 = unrelated guardians). From this roster I created a set of four dummy variables: two-parent family (including all families in which children lived with both of their biological or adoptive parents), stepfamily, single-parent family, and other family form. In an effort to simplify the analyses, I estimated a sample of statistical models with this full set of dummy variables and with only a single binary variable differentiating the two-parent families from all others. The results were similar across these two iterations, and so the final models presented in this book contained only the single binary marker.

Finally, parents responded to a series of questions about their own current employment and the employment of their children's other custodial parent. I collapsed these responses into a set of dummy variables for maternal employment status: mother working full-time (35 or more hours per week, following NCES guidelines), mother working part-time (fewer than 35 hours per week), mother not working, no mother present in the home, and mother missing employment information (about 10% of the sample). The same set of dummy variables was created for paternal employment status.

Math Learning   At each data collection, children took timed, computer-assisted achievement tests in math, reading, and general knowledge (e.g., social studies). As discussed in the opening chapter of this book, I chose to focus exclusively on the math tests as the marker of early learning in elementary school. This math test included items on conceptual knowledge, problem solving, number properties and operations, number sense, measurement, and the relations between numbers. Children took the first stage of the math test and then, based on their performance, took a second test for the low-, medium-, or high-difficulty stage. Item response theory (IRT) allowed the development of single proficiency scores across test sequences. These IRT scores placed children on a continuum of ability based on their correct, incorrect, and omitted responses on items of varying degrees of difficulty. IRT scores are directly comparable across data points, even as tests change. Thus an increase in IRT scores between kindergarten and first grade indicates significant movement along the ability continuum, despite the fact that the two tests at the basis of this comparison were different. Consequently, the mean IRT scores in the sample grow substantially from year to year.[6]

Of note is that the full set of IRT scores for all grades was reestimated with each data collection and release. In other words, the IRT scores for first-grade math released with the kindergarten/first-grade data in 2002 were not exactly the same as the IRT scores for first-grade math released with the kindergarten/first-grade/third-grade data in 2004. The reason for this somewhat disconcerting change is that the estimation of IRT scores, which after all are assessments of general ability, becomes more accurate with the accumulation of more data. In other words, analysis of three math tests allows a better estimation of ability at any one time point than the analysis of two math tests. Thus each release of data provides better data for math learning. The IRT scores in this study were all drawn from the most recent data release in 2004.

Another important consideration concerns language. Because English-language difficulties could potentially affect children's test performance, the NCES developed and administered the Oral Language Development Scale (OLDS), an extrapolation of the preLAS 2000 assessment,[7] to all ECLS-K children whose parents reported that English was not their primary language. In any given data collection, Spanish speakers who fell below a certain threshold on this scale took Spanish-language versions of the math tests but were excluded from the reading and general knowledge assessments. All non-Spanish speakers who fell below the threshold were excluded from all three assessments.

Although understandable, this strategy did slightly bias the Asian-American portion of the ECLS-K sample toward more assimilated children and families and created an important difference in the testing experiences of all children from Mexican immigrant families and all other Latino/a children. Although the small Asian-American bias is not correctable in the ECLS-K, the problem with the Spanish-speaking populations was addressed by including a binary marker of language assessment status in all models of math learning.

Control Variables   I have already discussed one control variable that was included in all multivariate analyses: non-Mexican immigrant status. Also included was a set of control variables provided by the NCES: a binary marker of sex, a continuous measure of age at the first point of data collection in years and months, a set of dummy variables designating geographic region (West, South, Midwest, Northeast), and a set of dummy variables designating residential urbanicity. For urbanicity I followed the lead of Lee and Burkham[8] and collapsed the original NCES-provided categories into a more manageable set of three (small town/rural, city fringe/large town, central city).

Domain and Context Measures

Chapters 3 and 4 are organized around specific sets of analyses focusing on different domains and contexts of development. Here, I describe each of the measures corresponding to these domains and contexts.

Physical Health   Four measures of health—two physical and two mental—were studied. Parents offered a global assessment of the physical health of their children on a five-point scale (1 = poor; 2 = fair; 3 = good; 4 = very good; 5 = excellent). These reports were reverse-coded to create the final scale of poor physical health. I should note that such global ratings are a common technique in health research, especially national-level health research, and that they have been demonstrated repeatedly to have high levels of validity and reliability.[9] The second physical health measure was based on work from leading adolescent health researchers in the immigration field, who have used counts of physical health problems to assess the relative health and well-being of immigrant youth.[10] To adapt this approach to the ECLS-K, I tapped four acute complications that were moderately intercorrelated. I first converted children's interviewer-measured height and weight to a body mass index (BMI). With the sex $\times$ age tables provided by the Centers for Disease Control and Prevention,[11] I then created a binary measure of overweight status (1 = BMI at or above the 85th percentile for age and sex; 0 = BMI be-low this threshold). Next, parents reported whether their children had expe-rienced frequent ear infections or untreated vision or hearing problems in the last year (1 = yes; 0 = no). These four binary items were summed to create a single scale.

In the child development literature internalizing and externalizing symp-tomatology are two of the most commonly studied aspects of mental health.[12] At each data point teachers completed a set of ratings about each target child as part of the social rating scale (SRS). Although children's scores on the SRS sub-scales are publicly available to ECLS-K researchers, the actual questionnaires used to create these scales are not. Thus I can provide only a general overview of these scales here. Children's scores on the internalizing subscale measured how often teachers observed signs of internalized distress scale (e.g., anxiety, loneliness, low self-esteem, and sadness), where a rating of 1 indicated that the teacher had never witnessed any such signs and a rating of 4 indicated that she or he had witnessed such signs very often. The externalizing subscale used the same 4-point rating to gauge how often teachers had observed signs of acting-out behaviors, including instances in which children argued, fought, got angry, acted impulsively, or disturbed others' activities (see Chapter 3 as well as my 2005 article in *American Educational Research Journal*[13] for a lengthier discus-sion of the pros and cons of using teacher reports in the assessment of child outcomes).

Three additional health-related measures were included in all health mod-els. All three were created with parent-reported data from the spring semester of kindergarten. First, health coverage and care was a summed scale of three binary items (1 = yes; 0 = no): whether the child was covered by a health in-surance plan, whether the child had visited a doctor in the last year for routine health care, and whether the child had visited a dentist in the last year for rou-tine care. Second, parental physical health was self-rated (1 = poor; 2 = fair; 3 = good; 4 = very good; 5 = excellent). Third, parental depression was based on a condensed version of the Center for Epidemiologic Studies–Depression (CES-D) scale.[14] Parents reported how often, during the past week, they had ex-perienced 11 depressive symptoms, such as loss of appetite, sleep disturbances, and fearfulness. Responses (1 = never; 2 = some of the time; 3 = a moderate amount of time; 4 = most of the time) were averaged to create the final scale (α = 0.85).

Psychosocial Measures   Both of the measures for psychosocial development—the approaches-to-learning scale to measure self-regulation and the interpersonal scale to measure social competence—were described in adequate detail in Chapter 2. Please note the discussion in this Appendix about the pros and cons of using such teacher reports.

Cognitive Measures   The kindergarten tests (and language screens) described here provided measures for the two indicators of cognitive development in this study. Children's IRT scores on the math achievement test in the fall semester of kindergarten served as the measure of preschool math skills. This measure was continuous and ranged from 6 to 98. The English-language screen attached to this fall-semester kindergarten test administration was used to create a binary marker of low English proficiency (1 = child scored below preset threshold on the language screen at the fall-semester kindergarten data collection; 0 = child did not have to take language screen or scored above the preset threshold).

Family Measures   I can give a little more detail here about the measurement of the four family factors than I did in the text of Chapter 4. First, parents assessed, on a 4-point scale (1 = never; 2 = sometimes; 3 = often; 4 = very often), how often they spoke a non-English language with their children. This report, which was taken during the data collection in the fall semester of kindergarten, served as my measure of non-English home language use. Second, I drew on the work of Katherine Magnuson and her colleagues[15] to create two scales tapping aspects of the home learning environment, as determined from the parent interviews conducted in the fall semester of kindergarten. Parents rated how often they engaged in a series of activities with their children, including building things, exploring nature, working with art, singing songs, playing games, and doing chores. This scale had four points: 1 = not at all; 2 = once or twice a week; 3 = three to six times a week; 4 = everyday. I took the average of these seven ratings to measure home learning activities ($\alpha = 0.67$). In this same battery parents also reported how often their children looked at picture books and reading books at home. I took the average of these two ratings to measure home reading activities ($r = 0.62$). Third, parents gave a yes/no answer to seven questions about their participation at their children's schools: whether they had attended a PTA meeting, parental advisory meeting, school event, parent-teacher conference, or open house event and whether they had volunteered at school or participated in fundraising activities in the past year. Parents received 1 point for every yes answer; I then took the sum of these points for each family, so that high scores on this scale indicated involved parents ($\alpha = 0.72$). Unlike the other three family measures, this measure was based on data collected during the spring semester (rather than the fall semester) of kindergarten.

Early Child Care Measures   The different types of early child care were measured by a set of dummy variables, adequately described in Chapter 4.

School Measures   Each of the six school measures was based on the reports of a school administrator (typically a principal) or of a classroom teacher. Although all other developmental domains and contexts were assessed in one of the two data collections in kindergarten, these administrator and teacher reports were taken during the spring semester of first grade. Beginning with the two school structure measures, the NCES broke down administrators' reports of total enrollment into a 5-point scale of school size (1 = 0–149; 2 = 150–299; 3 = 300–499; 4 = 500–749; 5 = 750+). Teachers in each school reported the number of years in which they had taught in their current schools and in first grade. These reports were standardized, averaged, and reverse-coded to create a measure of low teacher experience that ranged from a low of 0 to a high of 9.2.

For the school composition measures administrators estimated the percentage of students, in whole numbers (e.g., 42 = 42%), who were members of minority populations. These estimates served as the measure of school minority representation. Parent reports of household size and annual family income allowed the identification of all children from families below the federal poverty line. Drawing on aggregation techniques, I calculated the percentage of children in each representative in-school sample who met this criterion.

The two climate measures were replications of measures created by Lee and Burkham[16] with the ECLS-K data. For disorganized community location school administrators assessed the degree to which seven problems occurred in the neighborhoods surrounding their schools (1 = no problem; 2 = somewhat of a problem; 3 = big problem): (1) ethnic or religious differences, (2) excessive litter in the streets, (3) public drinking or drug use, (4) heavy traffic, (5) violent crimes, (6) vacant houses or buildings, and (7) general crime ($\alpha = 0.82$). Following the lead of Lee and Burkham, I took the mean of the seven items and then broke up the values into four categories: 1 (1) = none;

2 (1−1.5) = slight; 3 (1.5−2.0) = small;, and 4 (2.0+) = somewhat or big. School administrators also reported how often in the past year children had brought weapons to school, things had been taken from children or teachers by force at or around school, and children or teachers had been physically attacked (1 = yes; 0 = no). The sum of these responses (α = 0.57) measured safety problems at school.

In Chapter 5, I analyzed three other school-related variables in relation to math learning to guard against the finding of spurious associations between the six school characteristics of interest and math learning and to minimize the potential bias of teacher ratings of child outcomes by accounting for teachers' similarities to and familiarity with children from Mexican immigrant families. The first two variables were reported by school administrators: school sector (1 = private; 0 = public) and services for families with low English proficiency (a count of whether the school offered translators to parents, written translation of school communication, home visits to parents with low English proficiency, outreach programs to encourage involvement, non-English parent-teacher meetings, and other services). The third variable came from teachers who reported on the target student: teacher Latino/a status (1 = Latino/a; 0 = other race or ethnicity).

Description of Multivariate Analysis of the ECLS-K Data

Chapters 3 and 4 involved the analysis of racial/ethnic and immigration-related differences in measures from the three developmental domains and three developmental contexts. With the exception of the school analysis in Chapter 4 (explained later), these analyses followed the same format. In the first step the outcome was regressed on the set of racial/ethnic and immigrant status dummy variables and on the set of control variables—sex, age, non-Mexican immigrant status, region (with West as the omitted category), and urbanicity (with small town/rural as the omitted category). The results of this model estimated the baseline racial/ethnic and immigration-related differences in the outcome. In the second step the set of socioeconomic characteristics—family socioeconomic status, family poverty status, two-parent family structure, maternal employment (with no maternal employment as the omitted category), and paternal employment (with no paternal employment as the omitted category)—was added to this baseline model. These results disentangled racial/ethnic and immigration-related differences in the outcome from the highly correlated socioeconomic differences in this outcome.

Chapter 5 involved the analysis of racial/ethnic and immigration-related differences in math learning. Again, these analyses followed a similar format. In the first step the outcome was regressed on the set of racial/ethnic and immigrant status dummy variables and on the set of control variables. Inspection of changes in the unstandardized b coefficients for the racial/ethnic and immigrant status dummy variables revealed the extent to which corresponding socioeconomic status differences explained any observed racial/ethnic and immigration-related differences in first-grade math learning. Inspection of standardized β coefficients for all variables in the model allowed the assessment of which significant predictors of first-grade math learning had the greatest magnitude. In subsequent steps the baseline model incorporated, respectively, the family socioeconomic characteristics, the three sets of factors covering the developmental domains, and the three sets of factors covering the developmental contexts. In the final step I regressed the first-grade math IRT score on the full set of independent variables. Because this final model included the math IRT score from the fall semester of kindergarten as a predictor of the math IRT score from the spring semester of first grade, it effectively estimated changes in math learning between the start of kindergarten and the end of first grade. By shifting the focus from first grade to third grade, these analyses also controlled for the first-grade score. Therefore all third-grade models in Chapter 5 estimated changes in (or gains in) math test scores between first grade and third grade.

For the most part (again, the school context analyses being the exception), the multivariate analyses in this study were conducted with the mixed procedure in SAS, a type of multilevel modeling that partitions the variation in any given outcome into between-school and within-school components.[17] This procedure was highly valuable to this study for several reasons. First, the ECLS-K had a complex sampling frame, in which children were clustered in schools. Because two children in the same school were probably more similar than two children randomly drawn from the U.S. population, this frame violated assumptions of independence, leading to deflation of standard errors and corresponding inflation of probability levels. The partitioning of variation in the mixed procedure corrects that violation. Second, the mixed procedure can easily incorporate sampling weights, which are necessary for the accurate analysis of ECLS-K data because of its oversampling of some child groups and its nonrandom patterns of attrition and missing data. Third, some models in this study contained school-level variables as predictors of individual-level outcomes, and multilevel modeling is the best available method for accurately estimating such cross-level associations.

Having provided a general blueprint for the multivariate analyses in this study, now let me describe the exceptions to this general rule. For example, the health analyses involved two slight deviations from this format. First, these models contained three control variables (health coverage and care, parental physical health, parental depression) that were not included in the analysis of any other developmental domain or context. The reason for this addition had more to do with the analysis of math learning than the analysis of health. Any observed connection between child health and math learning could be a function of these dimensions of family health and well-being, and so these other dimensions must be controlled to account for this possibility.[18] For the sake of consistency, I also included these three control variables in the models in which the health factors served as outcomes. Second, the health problems outcome was a count variable. Consequently, I reestimated the health problems model using Poisson regression in STATA (with a robust standard error estimator). The results of this model did not differ significantly from the main multilevel models presented in this book.

In two cases (cognitive analyses and child care analyses) nonlinear outcomes required a shift in approach. The English-language outcome was binary, as were the different child care outcomes. Consequently, linear estimation was problematic, and I had to turn to logistic regression with the glimmix macro. This SAS technique converted the mixed procedure to nonlinear estimation techniques. These logistic models, however, followed the standard blueprint of all the domain and context models in Chapters 3 and 4.

As already mentioned, the school context analyses in Chapter 4 were the major exception to the general analytical blueprint. Unlike the other outcomes in Chapter 3 and Chapter 4, the school context characteristics were not measured on the individual level. Indeed, predicting school-level outcomes by individual-level outcomes is not appropriate. Instead, I turned to an alternative modeling strategy to assess racial/ethnic and immigration-related differences in school context and whether these differences were actually a function of corresponding differences in family socioeconomic status. Specifically, I worked with propensity scores.

Propensity scores are an attempt to adapt experimental designs to observational data. Unlike the experimental designs, observational data complicate the analysis of treatment effects because they do not normally allow randomized assignment to treatment and control groups. Thus group differences on some variable (the observed treatment effect) could be a function of differences on some other variable related to being in one group or the other. The best remedy for this bias is the control of potentially confounding factors (e.g., comparing groups that are similar but for the variable of interest). Propensity score matching is an efficient way to achieve this remedy because it uses a single index—the propensity score—to summarize information across potential confounding variables. Specifically, a propensity score is a conditional probability of individuals being in the treatment group given their pretreatment characteristics. Differences between individuals with the same or similar propensity score values should therefore be a function of the treatment and not of the characteristics associated with receiving the treatment.[19]

In this study Mexican immigrant status was the treatment, school context the outcome, and socioeconomic characteristics the potential confounding variables. Specifically, I used two sets of propensity scores. The first cataloged the basic control variables, and the second cataloged the basic control variables plus the socioeconomic variables (family socioeconomic status, family poverty, family structure, maternal employment status).

To generate these scores, I first created a subsample of children from Mexican immigrant families and their White peers, estimated a logistic regression to predict Mexican immigrant status by using the basic control variables in STATA, and then estimated a logistic regression to predict Mexican immigrant status by using the basic control variables plus the socioeconomic variables. Obviously, predicting Mexican immigrant status is a statistical sleight of hand. In reality, these regressions measured the individual or family characteristics of the average Mexican immigrant child to identify White children who looked like Mexican immigrant children according to two separate criteria. From these regressions I outputted the estimated probability of a respondent being in the focal category of the outcome—in other words, the odds of a child being from a Mexican immigrant family (vs. White)—given her or his values on the control variables and then outputted the estimated probability based on her or his values on the control variables plus the socioeconomic characteristics. These odds values became the propensity scores on which Mexican immigrant and White children were matched.

The average treatment—the kernel procedure in STATA—then used these propensity scores to compare Mexican immigrant and White children on their mean levels of the six school characteristics in two stages. In the first stage children from Mexican immigrant families were compared only to Whites with similar values on all the control variables, as captured by similar values on the first type of propensity score. In the second stage children from Mexican immigrant families were compared only to Whites with similar values on all the control variables and on all the family socioeconomic variables, as captured by similar values on the second type of propensity score. This same procedure was then repeated to compare the children from Mexican immigrant families to their African-American, Asian-American, and other Latino/a peers.[20]

This use of propensity scores brings up two additional issues. First, in the kernel method children from Mexican immigrant families were not matched to specific White (or other) children. Instead, they were matched to a weighted average of all White (or other) children, in which children's contribution to the weighted average was determined by their similarity to the Mexican immigrant child being matched. Second, bootstrapping techniques were required to produce the most accurate standard errors for the mean differences between comparison groups. For the comparison of each school characteristic between children from Mexican immigrant families and children from each of the four other racial or ethnic populations, therefore, standard errors were estimated with 1,000 bootstrap replications.[21]

Supplementary Presentation of Analytical Models

Table A2 is a near exact replication of Table 2.1 in Chapter 2. The only difference is that this table includes subscripts designating statistically significant racial/ethnic and immigration-related differences in the various factors listed in the table.

In each chapter I presented (either in figures or in the text) relatively straightforward results that were based on more complicated analyses. Specifically, I used three different methods of presentation.

First, for all linear analyses (most of the analyses in the book), I used predicted outcomes. To generate these predicted outcomes, I estimated what the score on the outcome of interest (say, poor physical health) would be for the average child in the sample (by multiplying each regression coefficient by the sample mean, summing these products, and then adding this sum to the intercept) and then adjusted this average score for each racial/ethnic and immigrant status population (by adding the coefficient for that population's dummy variable).

Second, for the analyses estimated with logistic rather than linear regression (e.g., English-language proficiency, early child care type), I discussed differences (compared to White children) in the odds of some outcome. These

Table A2 Breakdown of the Five Racial/Ethnic and Immigrant Populations in the ECLS-K, with Statistically Significant Population Differences Noted*

	Mexican Immigrant Family (%)	White (%)	African- American (%)	Other Latino/a (%)	Asian- American (%)
Demographic information					
Residence in South	27.05[c]	31.41[b]	60.88[a]	27.66[c]	13.82[d]
Residence in Northeast	2.08[d]	22.51[a]	15.04[c]	18.73[b]	12.44[c]
Residence in Midwest	6.89[d]	32.47[a]	16.04[b,c]	14.01[c]	17.66[b]
Residence in West	63.98[a]	13.60[d]	8.05[e]	39.60[c]	56.08[b]
Residence in large city	66.45[a]	28.92[e]	51.55[c]	56.06[b]	44.28[d]
Residence in suburb	29.91[c]	42.64[a]	34.52[b]	34.13[b]	35.86[b]
Residence in rural area	3.64[e]	28.43[a]	13.93[c]	9.81[d]	19.85[b]
Socioeconomic information					
Family in poverty	49.02[a]	7.86[e]	38.73[b]	25.96[c]	20.22[d]
Child lives with two married parents	78.67[a]	77.26[c]	33.13[c]	62.16[b]	78.87
Mother works full-time**	26.01[c]	38.62[b]	50.83[a]	41.29[b]	42.18[b]
Mother works part-time	11.57[c,d]	24.03[a]	10.99[d]	18.35[b]	14.09[c]
Mother not working	49.28[a]	26.45[b,c]	24.53[c]	29.35[b]	28.64[b]
No mother present	.65	1.34	1.39	1.57	1.56
Father works full-time**	65.80[b]	74.74[a]	33.52[d]	58.83[c]	66.79[b]
Father works part-time	4.03[a]	2.16[b]	1.66[b]	3.77[a]	3.75[a]
Father not working	4.81[a,b]	2.68[c]	4.27[b]	5.15[a,b]	5.95[a]
No father present	11.05[c]	10.58[c]	48.22[a]	22.38[b]	9.88[c]
Demographic information					
Average age (years)	6.15[e]	6.26[a]	6.20[c]	6.19[b]	6.14[c]
Socioeconomic information					
Average family socioeconomic status (-5 to 3)	-0.73[e]	0.26[a]	-0.35[d]	-0.24[c]	0.15[b]
Math achievement information					
Average fall kindergarten math score ($6-98$)	15.36[d]	24.11[a]	18.23[c]	18.91[b]	23.79[a]
Average spring first-grade math score ($8-108$)	47.12[d]	59.13[a]	47.24[d]	51.16[c]	55.27[b]
Average spring third-grade math score ($3-121$)	75.72[d]	89.43[a]	73.87[e]	81.08[c]	86.72[b]
n	769	7,748	1,802	1,586	1,093

* Means with different superscripts differ significantly ($p < 0.01$), as determined by post hoc ANOVA tests.

** For parental employment variables, a fifth category (missing employment information) is not shown.

[a]–[e] An "a" designates the largest mean, with smaller means designated in alphabetical order.

differences were assessed by exponentiating the b coefficients from the logistic models, subtracting 1 from these exponentiated odds ratios, and then multiplying the resulting number by 100.

Third, for the propensity score analyses I used the mean levels on the six school context variables for children from Mexican immigrant families and White families matched on the control variables and then again matched on the control variables plus the socioeconomic characteristics. Because the results for the propensity score analyses comparing children from Mexican immigrant families to children from the non-White populations were so similar to those in the Mexican-White comparison, I did not present the Mexican/non-White results in Chapter 4.

In what follows I present a series of tables. In these tables are the complete results of the linear, logistic, and propensity score models that were used to calculate the predicted outcomes, odds, and means that were presented in Chapters 3, 4, and 5.

Table A3 Results of Regression Models Predicting Two Dimensions of Physical Health

	Poor Physical Health				Physical Health Problems			
	Model 1		Model 2		Model 1		Model 2	
	b	SE	b	SE	b	SE	b	SE
Race/ethnicity and immigration status								
Mexican immigrant family	0.43***	0.04	0.26***	0.04	0.11***	0.03	0.07*	0.03
White[a]	–	–	–	–	–	–	–	–
African-American	0.19***	0.03	0.06*	0.03	0.05**	0.02	0.00	0.02
Asian-American	0.26***	0.05	0.22***	0.05	−0.03	0.04	−0.04	0.04
Latino/a	0.13***	0.03	0.05+	0.03	0.05*	0.03	0.02	0.02
Control variables								
Sex (female)	−0.08***	0.02	−0.08***	0.02	−0.03**	0.01	−0.02*	0.01
Age (years)	0.06**	0.02	0.05*	0.02	0.05**	0.02	0.05**	0.02
Non-Mexican immigrant family	0.05	0.03	0.07*	0.03	0.02	0.02	0.03	0.02
West[a]	–	–	–	–	–	–	–	–
South	0.03	0.04	0.03	0.03	0.01	0.03	0.00	0.03
Midwest	0.02	0.04	0.04	0.04	−0.02	0.03	−0.02	0.03
Northeast	−0.05	0.04	−0.03	0.04	0.05	0.03	0.06+	0.03
Small town/rural[a]	–	–	–	–	–	–	–	–
Large city	0.02	0.04	0.04	0.04	0.03	0.03	0.04	0.03
City fringe/large town	−0.06	0.04+	0.00	0.04+	0.00	0.03	0.02	0.03
Family socioeconomic factors								
Socioeconomic status	–	–	−0.07***	0.01	–	–	−0.05***	0.01
Family poverty status	–	–	0.08***	0.02	–	–	0.03+	0.02
Family structure (two-parent)	–	–	−0.04+	0.02	–	–	−0.02	0.02
Mother not working[a]	–	–	–	–	–	–	–	–
Mother working full-time	–	–	−0.01	0.02	–	–	0.03+	0.01
Mother working part-time	–	–	−0.07***	0.02	–	–	−0.06***	0.02
No mother present	–	–	−0.09	0.07	–	–	−0.06	0.05
Father not working[a]	–	–	–	–	–	–	–	–
Father working full-time	–	–	−0.05	0.04	–	–	−0.05+	0.03

Table A3 *Continued*

| | Poor Physical Health | | | | Physical Health Problems | | | |
| | Model 1 | | Model 2 | | Model 1 | | Model 2 | |
	b	*SE*	*b*	*SE*	*b*	*SE*	*b*	*SE*
Family socioeconomic factors (continued)								
Father working part-time	–	–	−0.03	0.06	–	–	−0.03	0.05
No father present	–	–	−0.03	0.04	–	–	−0.04	0.04
Additional health factors								
Health care and coverage	–	–	0.01	0.01	–	–	0.01	0.01
Parental physical health	–	–	−0.18***	0.01	–	–	−0.03***	0.00
Parental depression	–	–	0.06***	0.02	–	–	0.07***	0.01
Intercept	1.26***	0.14	1.96***	0.16	0.11	0.11	0.12	0.12
δ2 Res LL	–	–	−620		–	–	−68	

n = 10,602 (all models).

*** $p < 0.001$.

** $p < 0.01$.

* $p < 0.05$.

+ $p < 0.10$.

[a] Reference category for set of dummy variables (race/ethnicity and immigration status, region, urbanicity, maternal employment, paternal employment) The employment set of dummy variables also includes a binary marker for those missing employment information for either parent.

Table A4 Results of Regression Models Predicting Two Dimensions of Mental Health

	Internalizing Symptoms				Externalizing Symptoms			
	Model 1		Model 2		Model 1		Model 2	
	b	SE	b	SE	b	SE	b	SE
Race/ethnicity and immigration status								
Mexican immigrant family	−0.01	0.03	−0.05*	0.02	−0.06*	0.03	−0.09**	0.03
White[a]	−	−	−	−	−	−	−	−
African-American	0.07***	0.02	0.02	0.02	0.24***	0.04	0.15***	0.04
Asian-American	−0.06*	0.03	−0.06*	0.03	−0.13***	0.04	−0.14***	0.04
Latino/a	0.01	0.02	0.03+	0.01	0.01	0.02	−0.05*	0.02
Control variables								
Sex (female)	−0.04***	0.00	−0.04***	0.00	−0.27***	0.01	−0.26***	0.01
Age (years)	−0.02	0.01	−0.02	0.01	−0.07***	0.02	−0.08***	0.02
Non-Mexican immigrant family	−0.02	0.02	−0.01	0.02	−0.02	0.02	0.00	0.02
West[a]	−	−	−	−	−	−	−	−
South	−0.01	0.03	−0.02	0.03	0.03	0.03	0.01	0.03
Midwest	−0.03	0.03	−0.03	0.03	−0.03	0.03	−0.03	0.03
Northeast	0.00	0.03	0.01	0.03	−0.08*	0.03	−0.07+	0.03
Small town/rural[a]	−	−	−	−	−	−	−	−
Large city	0.03	0.03	0.04	0.03	0.02	0.03	0.02	0.03
City fringe/large town	0.03	0.03	0.06*	0.03	0.02	0.03	0.05	0.03
Family socioeconomic factors								
Socioeconomic status	−	−	−0.03**	0.01	−	−	−0.03***	0.00
Family poverty status	−	−	0.03+	0.02	−	−	0.03	0.02
Family structure (two-parent)	−	−	−0.11***	0.02	−	−	−0.20***	0.02
Mother not working[a]	−	−	−	−	−	−	−	−
Mother working full-time	−	−	−0.01	0.01	−	−	0.09***	0.01
Mother working part-time	−	−	0.00	0.01	−	−	0.03+	0.02
No mother present	−	−	0.21***	0.04	−	−	0.16***	0.05
Father not working[a]	−	−	−	−	−	−	−	−
Father working full-time	−	−	−0.09***	0.03	−	−	−0.05+	0.03
Father working part-time	−	−	−0.11**	0.04	−	−	−0.13**	0.05
No father present	−	−	−0.10***	0.03	−	−	−0.09**	0.03

Table A4 *Continued*

| | Internalizing Symptoms | | | | Externalizing Symptoms | | | |
| | Model 1 | | Model 2 | | Model 1 | | Model 2 | |
	b	*SE*	*b*	*SE*	*b*	*SE*	*b*	*SE*
Additional health factors								
Health care and coverage	–	–	−0.02*	0.01	–	–	−0.03*	0.01
Parental physical health	–	–	−0.03***	0.01	–	–	−0.02⁺	0.00
Parental depression	–	–	0.03**	0.01	–	–	0.06***	0.01
Intercept	1.67***	0.09	1.99***	0.10	2.23***	0.11	2.42***	0.12
δ *2 Res LL*	–	–	−188		–	–	−291	

$n = 10,602$ (all models).

*** $p < 0.001$.

** $p < 0.01$.

* $p < 0.05$.

⁺ $p < 0.10$.

[a] Reference category for set of dummy variables (race/ethnicity and immigration status, region, urbanicity, maternal employment, paternal employment). The employment set of dummy variables also includes a binary marker for those missing employment information for either parent.

Table A5 Results of Regression Models Predicting Two Dimensions of Psychosocial Development

	Self-Regulation				Social Competence			
	Model 1		Model 2		Model 1		Model 2	
	b	SE	b	SE	b	SE	b	SE
Race/ethnicity and immigration status								
Mexican immigrant family	−0.03	0.03	0.08*	0.03	−0.08*	0.03	−0.01	0.03
White[a]	−	−	−	−	−	−	−	−
African-American	−0.22***	0.02	−0.10***	0.02	−0.21***	0.02	−0.13***	0.02
Asian-American	0.08*	0.03	0.11**	0.03	−0.05	0.03	−0.03	0.03
Latino/a	−0.10***	0.02	−0.02	0.02	−0.08	0.02	−0.02	0.02
Control variables								
Sex (female)	0.30***	0.01	0.29***	0.01	0.22***	0.01	0.22***	0.01
Age (years)	0.28***	0.02	0.28***	0.02	0.09***	0.02	0.10***	0.02
Non-Mexican immigrant family	0.02	0.02	−0.01	0.02	−0.01	0.02	−0.03	0.02
West[a]	−	−	−	−	−	−	−	−
South	−0.05+	0.03	−0.03	0.03	0.03	0.03	0.05	0.03
Midwest	0.01	0.03	0.00	0.03	0.01	0.03	0.01	0.03
Northeast	0.02	0.03	0.01	0.03	0.05	0.03	0.04	0.03
Small town/rural[a]	−	−	−	−	−	−	−	−
Large city	−0.01	0.03	−0.02	0.03	−0.01	0.03	−0.02	0.03
City fringe/large town	−0.08**	0.03	0.03	0.03	0.04	0.03	0.00	0.03
Family socioeconomic factors								
Socioeconomic status	−	−	0.14***	0.01	−	−	0.09***	0.01
Family poverty status	−	−	−0.05**	0.02	−	−	−0.04*	0.02
Family structure (two-parent)	−	−	0.11***	0.02	−	−	0.09***	0.02
Mother not working[a]	−	−	−	−	−	−	−	−
Mother working full-time	−	−	−0.01	0.01	−	−	−0.04**	0.01
Mother working part-time	−	−	0.01	0.02	−	−	0.01	0.02
No mother present	−	−	−0.16**	0.05	−	−	0.02	0.05
Father not working[a]	−	−	−	−	−	−	−	−
Father working full-time	−	−	0.12***	0.03	−	−	0.08**	0.02

Table A5 *Continued*

	Self-Regulation				Social Competence			
	Model 1		Model 2		Model 1		Model 2	
	b	*SE*	*b*	*SE*	*b*	*SE*	*b*	*SE*
Family socioeconomic factors (continued)								
Father working part-time	–	–	0.12*	0.05	–	–	0.11*	0.04
No father present	–	–	0.07*	0.03	–	–	0.07*	0.03
Intercept	1.15***	0.11	0.91***	0.11	2.31***	0.11	2.15***	0.11
δ *2 Res LL*	–	–	−461		–	–	−226	

  n = 11,219 (all models).
  *** *p* < 0.001.
  ** *p* < 0.01.
  * *p* < 0.05.
  + *p* < 0.10.
  [a] Reference category for set of dummy variables (race/ethnicity and immigration status, region, urbanicity, maternal employment, paternal employment). The employment set of dummy variables also includes a binary marker for those missing employment information for either parent.

Table A6 Results of Regression Models Predicting Two Dimensions of Cognitive Development

| | Low English Proficiency (Binary) | | | | Kindergarten Math Score (Continuous) | | | |
| | Model 1 | | Model 2 | | Model 1 | | Model 2 | |
	b	SE	b	SE	b	SE	b	SE
Race/ethnicity and immigration status								
Mexican immigrant family	7.92***	0.39	7.43***	0.39	−6.27***	0.37	−4.11***	0.36
White[a]	−	−	−	−	−	−	−	−
African-American	0.92*	0.47	0.52	0.47	−4.15***	0.25	−2.43***	0.25
Asian-American	0.19	0.55	0.23	0.54	0.42	0.44	0.51	0.42
Latino/a	5.42***	0.39	5.18***	0.39	−4.09	0.25	−2.58	0.25
Control variables								
Sex (female)	0.10+	0.06	0.13*	0.06	0.15	0.14	0.07	0.13
Age (years)	−0.59***	0.09	−0.62***	0.09	5.61***	0.20	5.74***	0.19
Non-Mexican immigrant family	1.37***	0.09	1.39***	0.09	−0.21	0.29	−0.68*	0.27
West[a]	−	−	−	−	−	−	−	−
South	−0.46+	0.27	−0.49+	0.27	−0.23	0.41	0.10	0.35
Midwest	−1.81***	0.42	−1.82***	0.42	0.21	0.44	0.00	0.28
Northeast	−1.10***	0.34	−1.17***	0.34	0.90*	0.46	0.54	0.40
Small town/rural[a]	−	−	−	−	−	−	−	−
Large city	2.04***	0.46	2.29***	0.46	0.76+	0.42	0.55+	0.37
City fringe/large town	−1.16*	0.48	−1.66***	0.49	2.46***	0.42	1.51***	0.37
Family socioeconomic factors								
Socioeconomic status	−	−	−1.12***	0.07	−	−	3.26***	0.01
Family poverty status	−	−	0.62***	0.07	−	−	−0.20	0.02
Family structure (two-parent)	−	−	−0.45***	0.10	−	−	1.04***	0.02
Mother not working[a]	−	−	−	−	−	−	−	−
Mother working full-time	−	−	−0.41***	0.07	−	−	−0.02	0.17
Mother working part-time	−	−	−0.75***	0.09	−	−	0.49**	0.20
No mother present	−	−	−2.62***	0.34	−	−	0.54	0.58
Father not working[a]	−	−	−	−	−	−	−	−

Table A6 *Continued*

| | Low English Proficiency (Binary) | | | | Kindergarten Math Score (Continuous) | | | |
| | Model 1 | | Model 2 | | Model 1 | | Model 2 | |
	b	*SE*	*b*	*SE*	*b*	*SE*	*b*	*SE*
Family socioeconomic factors (continued)								
Father working full-time	–	–	−0.15	0.13	–	–	1.14**	0.36
Father working part-time	–	–	0.52**	0.19	–	–	1.55**	0.54
No father present	–	–	−1.22***	0.16	–	–	0.80*	0.40
Intercept	−6.61***	0.79	−6.14***	0.81	−13.22***	1.35	−15.91***	1.34
δ *2 Res LL*	–	–	−5670		–	–	−1119	

n = 11,219 (all models).
*** *p* < 0.001.
** *p* < 0.01.
* *p* < 0.05.
+ *p* < 0.10.
[a] Reference category for set of dummy variables (race/ethnicity and immigration status, region, urbanicity, maternal employment, paternal employment). The employment set of dummy variables also includes a binary marker for those missing employment information for either parent.

Table A7 Results of Regression Models Predicting Language Use and Parental Involvement in Education

| | Family Non-English-Language Use | | | | Parental Involvement in Education | | | |
| | Model 1 | | Model 2 | | Model 1 | | Model 2 | |
	b	SE	b	SE	b	SE	b	SE
Race/ethnicity and immigration status								
Mexican immigrant family	2.16***	0.03	2.06***	0.03	−0.80***	0.08	−0.46***	0.08
White[a]	−	−	−	−	−	−	−	−
African-American	−0.10***	0.02	−0.12***	0.02	−0.68***	0.05	−0.25***	0.05
Asian-American	0.63***	0.03	0.62***	0.03	−0.55***	0.09	−0.53***	0.08
Latino/a	0.78***	0.02	0.74***	0.02	−0.53***	0.05	−0.21***	0.05
Control variables								
Sex (female)	0.00	0.01	0.00	0.01	0.02	0.03	0.01	0.03
Age (years)	−0.01	0.02	−0.02	0.01	−0.05	0.04	0.00	0.04
Non-Mexican immigrant family	0.81***	0.02	0.81***	0.02	−0.27***	0.06	−0.40***	0.06
West[a]	−	−	−	−	−	−	−	−
South	0.00	0.03	−0.01	0.03	−0.19*	0.08	−0.10	0.07
Midwest	−0.02	0.03	−0.01	0.03	−0.02	0.09	−0.04	0.08
Northeast	0.03	0.03	0.04	0.03	−0.25**	0.09	−0.33**	0.08
Small town/rural[a]	−	−	−	−	−	−	−	−
Large city	0.16***	0.02	0.17***	0.03	0.05	0.08	0.02	0.07
City fringe/large town	0.05+	0.02	0.08*	0.02	0.37***	0.08	0.16*	0.07
Family socioeconomic factors								
Socioeconomic status	−	−	−0.07***	0.01	−	−	0.58***	0.02
Family poverty	−	−	0.08***	0.02	−	−	−0.01	0.04
Family structure (two-parent)	−	−	0.01	0.02	−	−	0.91***	0.04
Mother not working[a]	−	−	−	−	−	−	−	−
Mother working full-time	−	−	−0.04***	0.01	−	−	−0.08*	0.03
Mother working part-time	−	−	−0.04**	0.01	−	−	0.19***	0.04
No mother present	−	−	−0.17***	0.04	−	−	0.15	0.12
Father not working[a]	−	−	−	−	−	−	−	−

Table A7 *Continued*

	Family Non-English-Language Use				Parental Involvement in Education			
	Model 1		Model 2		Model 1		Model 2	
	b	*SE*	*b*	*SE*	*b*	*SE*	*b*	*SE*
Family socioeconomic factors (continued)								
Father working full-time	–	–	−0.01	0.03	–	–	0.31***	0.07
Father working part-time	–	–	−0.02	0.04	–	–	−0.02	0.11
No father present	–	–	−0.06*	0.03	–	–	0.57***	0.08
Intercept	1.09***	0.09	1.14***	0.10	4.11***	0.28	2.83***	0.27
δ *2 R.es LL*	–	–	−109		–	–	−1573	

$n = 11{,}558$ (all models).

*** $p < 0.001$.

** $p < 0.01$.

* $p < 0.05$.

+ $p < 0.10$.

[a] Reference category for set of dummy variables (race/ethnicity and immigration status, region, urbanicity, maternal employment, paternal employment). The employment set of dummy variables also includes a binary marker for those missing employment information for either parent.

Table A8 Results of Regression Models Predicting Two Dimensions of Learning Activity at Home

	Home Learning Activities				Home Reading Activities			
	Model 1		Model 2		Model 1		Model 2	
	b	SE	b	SE	b	SE	b	SE
Race/ethnicity and immigration status								
Mexican immigrant family	−0.34***	0.02	−0.30***	0.03	−0.38***	0.03	−0.32***	0.04
White[a]	–	–	–	–	–	–	–	–
African-American	0.02	0.02	0.06***	0.02	0.02	0.02	0.07**	0.02
Asian-American	−0.03	0.03	−0.03	0.03	−0.02	0.04	−0.02	0.04
Latino/a	−0.06***	0.02	−0.03	0.02	−0.11***	0.02	−0.06**	0.02
Control variables								
Sex (female)	−0.03**	0.01	−0.03**	0.01	0.31***	0.01	0.31***	0.01
Age (years)	−0.04**	0.01	−0.04**	0.01	−0.09***	0.02	−0.09***	0.02
Non-Mexican immigrant family	−0.12***	0.02	−0.14***	0.02	−0.04	0.03	−0.05[+]	0.03
West[a]	–	–	–	–	–	–	–	–
South	0.03	0.02	−0.03	0.02	−0.05[+]	0.03	−0.05	0.03
Midwest	−0.02	0.02	−0.02	0.02	−0.06[+]	0.03	−0.06[+]	0.03
Northeast	−0.03	0.02	−0.04	0.02	−0.01	0.03	−0.02	0.03
Small town/rural[a]	–	–	–	–	–	–	–	–
Large city	−0.03	0.02	−0.04[+]	0.02	0.02	0.03	0.01	0.03
City fringe/ large town	0.00	0.02	−0.02	0.02	0.00	0.03	−0.03	0.03
Family socioeconomic factors								
Socioeconomic status	–	–	0.07***	0.01	–	–	0.09***	0.01
Family poverty status	–	–	0.01	0.01	–	–	0.01	0.02
Family structure (two-parent)	–	–	0.03*	0.01	–	–	−0.02	0.02
Mother not working[a]	–	–	–	–	–	–	–	–
Mother working full-time	–	–	−0.05***	0.01	–	–	−0.03*	0.02
Mother working part-time	–	–	−0.04***	0.01	–	–	−0.03	0.02
No mother present	–	–	−0.02	0.04	–	–	−0.13*	0.06
Father not working[a]	–	–	–	–	–	–	–	–

Table A8 *Continued*

	Home Learning Activities				Home Reading Activities			
	Model 1		*Model 2*		*Model 1*		*Model 2*	
	b	*SE*	*b*	*SE*	*b*	*SE*	*b*	*SE*
Family socioeconomic factors (continued)								
Father working full-time	–	–	0.00	0.02	–	–	0.06*	0.03
Father working part-time	–	–	0.02	0.04	–	–	0.05	0.05
No father present	–	–	0.00	0.03	–	–	−0.01	0.04
Intercept	3.05***	0.09	3.06***	0.09	3.63***	0.12	3.60***	0.13
δ *2 Res LL*	–	–	−65		–	–	−57	

$n = 11,558$ (all models).

*** $p < 0.001$.

** $p < 0.01$.

* $p < 0.05$.

+ $p < 0.10$.

[a] Reference category for set of dummy variables (race/ethnicity and immigration status, region, urbanicity, maternal employment, paternal employment). The employment set of dummy variables also includes a binary marker for those missing employment information for either parent.

Table A9 Results of Logistic Regression Models Predicting Two Types of Home-Based Early Child Care

	Parental Care				Nonparental Home-Based Care			
	Model 1		Model 2		Model 1		Model 2	
	b	SE	b	SE	b	SE	b	SE
Race/ethnicity and immigration status								
Mexican immigrant family	1.03***	0.10	0.35**	0.11	−0.18+	0.11	−0.20+	0.12
White[a]	−	−	−	−	−	−	−	−
African-American	−0.32***	0.09	−0.30**	0.10	−0.05	0.07	−0.25**	0.08
Asian-American	0.26*	0.11	0.36**	0.11	−0.07	0.11	−0.06	0.11
Latino/a	0.32***	0.08	0.18*	0.09	0.11	0.07	0.09	0.08
Control variables								
Sex (female)	−0.09+	0.05	−0.11*	0.05	0.04	0.04	0.05	0.05
Age (years)	0.10	0.07	0.08	0.07	−0.18**	0.06	−0.17*	0.06
Non-Mexican immigrant family	0.21*	0.08	0.19*	0.09	−0.21*	0.09	−0.14*	0.09
West[a]	−	−	−	−	−	−	−	−
South	−0.07	0.09	−0.14	0.09	−0.25***	0.08	−0.31***	0.08
Midwest	−0.29**	0.10	−0.29**	0.10	0.29***	0.08	0.29***	0.08
Northeast	−0.09	0.09	−0.16	0.10	0.09	0.08	0.16+	0.08
Small town/rural[a]	−	−	−	−	−	−	−	−
Large city	−0.12	0.09	−0.01	0.09	−0.36***	0.07	−0.35***	0.07
City fringe/large town	−0.18*	0.09	−0.08	0.09	−0.41***	0.07	−0.37***	0.07
Family socioeconomic factors								
Socioeconomic status	−	−	−0.62***	0.04	−	−	−0.05	0.03
Family poverty status	−	−	−0.14+	0.08	−	−		0.08
Family structure (two-parent)	−	−	0.40***	0.08	−	−		0.07
Mother not working[a]	−	−	−	−	−	−	−	−
Mother working full-time	−	−	−1.43***	0.06	−	−	1.75***	0.07
Mother working part-time	−	−	−0.82***	0.07	−	−	1.15***	0.08

Table A9 *Continued*

	Parental Care				Nonparental Home-Based Care			
	Model 1		Model 2		Model 1		Model 2	
	b	*SE*	*b*	*SE*	*b*	*SE*	*b*	*SE*
Family socioeconomic factors (continued)								
No mother present	–	–	−1.56***	0.27	–	–	1.60***	0.18
Father not working[a]	–	–	–	–	–	–	–	–
Father working full-time	–	–	−0.32*	0.12	–	–	0.46***	0.13
Father working part-time	–	–	−0.22*	0.18	–	–	0.18	0.19
No father present	–	–	−0.53***	0.14	–	–	0.47**	0.15
Intercept	−2.10***	0.43	−1.10*	0.47	0.23	0.39	−1.33**	0.44
δ *2 Res LL*	–	–	−2714		–	–	−2369	

$n = 11,588$ (all models).

*** $p < 0.001$.

** $p < 0.01$.

* $p < 0.05$.

+ $p < 0.10$.

[a] Reference category for set of dummy variables (race/ethnicity and immigration status, region, urbanicity, maternal employment, paternal employment). The employment set of dummy variables also includes a binary marker for those missing employment information for either parent.

Table A10 Results of Logistic Regression Models Predicting Two Types of Center-Based Early Child Care

	Preschool				Day Care Center			
	Model 1		Model 2		Model 1		Model 2	
	b	SE	b	SE	b	SE	b	SE
Race/ethnicity and immigration status								
Mexican immigrant family	−1.21***	0.12	−0.77***	0.12	−1.05***	0.24	−0.58*	0.24
White[a]	−	−	−	−	−	−	−	−
African-American	−0.89***	0.08	−0.35***	0.08	0.22*	0.10	0.13	0.11
Asian-American	−0.30**	0.10	−0.16+	0.10	−0.65***	0.19	−0.66***	0.19
Latino/a	−0.73***	0.08	−0.39***	0.08	−0.08	0.11	−0.02	0.12
Control variables								
Sex (female)	0.01	0.04	0.01	0.04	−0.08	0.06	−0.08	0.06
Age (years)	0.14*	0.06	0.18**	0.06	−0.27**	0.09	−0.24*	0.10
Non-Mexican immigrant family	0.06	0.07	−0.02	0.08	0.09	0.12	0.15	0.13
West[a]	−	−	−	−	−	−	−	−
South	0.09	0.09	0.15+	0.08	0.56***	0.13	0.54***	0.13
Midwest	−0.04	0.09	−0.11	0.09	0.39**	0.14	0.39**	0.14
Northeast	−0.07	0.08	−0.15+	0.08	0.41**	0.14	0.47**	0.14
Small town/rural[a]	−	−	−	−	−	−	−	−
Large city	0.76***	0.09	0.66***	0.08	0.06	0.12	0.04	0.12
City fringe/ large town	0.90***	0.09	0.68***	0.08	−0.08	0.12	−0.08	0.12
Family socioeconomic factors								
Socioeconomic status	−	−	0.50***	0.03	−	−	0.23***	0.05
Family poverty status	−	−	−0.52***	0.08	−	−	0.01	0.11
Family structure (two-parent)	−	−	0.31***	0.07	−	−	−0.17	0.10
Mother not working[a]	−	−	−	−	−	−	−	−
Mother working full-time	−	−	−0.62***	0.05	−	−	1.54***	0.10
Mother working part-time	−	−	−0.23***	0.06	−	−	0.88***	0.12
No mother present	−	−	−0.92***	0.21	−	−	1.40***	0.27

Table A10 *Continued*

	Preschool				Day Care Center			
	Model 1		Model 2		Model 1		Model 2	
	b	*SE*	*b*	*SE*	*b*	*SE*	*b*	*SE*
Family socioeconomic factors (continued)								
Father not working[a]	–	–	–	–	–	–	–	–
Father working full-time	–	–	0.12	0.12	–	–	0.11	0.19
Father working part-time	–	–	0.11	0.17	–	–	0.09	0.28
No father present	–	–	0.08	0.14	–	–	0.36[+]	0.21
Intercept	−1.87***	0.38	−2.03***	0.41	−1.37***	0.59	−2.65***	0.65
δ *2 Res LL*	–	–	−1287		–	–	−2713	

$n = 11,588$ (all models).

*** $p < 0.001$.

** $p < 0.01$.

* $p < 0.05$.

+ $p < 0.10$.

[a] Reference category for set of dummy variables (race/ethnicity and immigration status, region, urbanicity, maternal employment, paternal employment). The employment set of dummy variables also includes a binary marker for those missing employment information for either parent.

Table A11 Mean School Characteristics for Children from Mexican Immigrant Families and Other Racial/Ethnic Populations

	Mean for Unmatched on Family Socioeconomic Status[a]			Mean for Matched on Family Socioeconomic Status[b]		
	Comparison Group	Significance	Mexican Immigrant	Comparison Group	Significance	Mexican Immigrant
Native White vs. Mexican immigrant						
School size (1–5)	3.36	***	4.14	3.44	***	4.16
Low teacher experience (0–9.2)	7.25	***	7.94	7.31	**	7.94
Minority representation (0–100)	25.97	***	80.63	30.69	***	80.67
Proportion of student body in poverty (0–1)	0.09	***	0.39	0.20	***	0.39
Disorganized community location (1–4)	1.89	***	2.81	2.01	***	2.81
Safety problems in school (0–3)	0.44	***	0.55	0.46	+	0.55
Native African-American vs. Mexican immigrant						
School size (1–5)	3.56	***	4.16	3.67	***	4.15
Low teacher experience (0–9.2)	7.67	***	7.94	7.70	*	7.93
Minority representation (0–100)	69.89	***	80.63	71.10	**	80.67
Proportion of student body in poverty (0–1)	0.24	***	0.39	0.30	***	0.39
Disorganized community location (1–4)	2.41	***	2.81	2.28	**	2.81
Safety problems in school (0–3)	0.68	**	0.55	0.81	***	0.55
Native Asian-American vs. Mexican immigrant						
School size (1–5)	3.77	***	4.16	3.97	**	4.16
Low teacher experience (0–9.2)	7.45	***	7.90	7.17	***	7.90
Minority representation (0–100)	55.78	***	80.63	65.11	***	80.67
Proportion of student body in poverty (0–1)	0.16	***	0.39	0.31	***	0.39
Disorganized community location (1–4)	2.09	***	2.63	2.27	***	2.63
Safety problems in school (0–3)	0.50	n.s.	0.54	0.57	n.s.	0.55

Table A11 *Continued*

	Mean for Unmatched on Family Socioeconomic Status[a]			Mean for Matched on Family Socioeconomic Status[b]		
	Comparison Group	Significance	Mexican Immigrant	Comparison Group	Significance	Mexican Immigrant
Native Latino/a vs. Mexican immigrant						
School size (1–5)	3.68	***	4.16	3.87	***	4.15
Low teacher experience (0–9.2)	7.55	***	7.94	7.64	**	7.93
Minority representation (0–100)	59.33	***	80.63	69.66	***	80.67
Proportion of student body in poverty (0–1)	0.22	***	0.39	0.32	***	0.39
Disorganized community location (1–4)	2.41	***	2.81	2.66	**	2.81
Safety problems in school (0–3)	0.50	n.s.	0.54	0.61	n.s.	0.55

$n = 769$ (Mexican immigrant), 7,748 (White), 1,802 (African-American), 1,093 (Asian-American), 1,591 (other Latino/a).

*** Mean level of school characteristic differs significantly ($p < 0.001$) across two groups, as determined by pooled t tests.

** $p < 0.01$.

* $p < 0.05$.

[+] $p < 0.10$.

n.s. = Nonsignificant.

[a] Propensity score cataloged the control variables (sex, age, immigrant status, region, urbanicity).

[b] Propensity score cataloged the control variables and the family socioeconomic variables (family socioeconomic status, family poverty, family structure, maternal employment, paternal employment).

Table A12 Results of Regression Models Predicting Math Achievement in First Grade by Various Developmental Domains and Contexts

	Model 1		Model 2		Model 3		Model 4	
	b	SE	b	SE	b	SE	b	SE
Race/ethnicity and immigration status								
Mexican immigrant family	−9.81***	0.79	−5.51***	0.78	−8.68***	0.77	−9.43***	0.72
White[a]	−	−	−	−	−	−	−	−
African-American	−9.69***	0.51	−7.00***	0.51	−8.35***	0.50	−7.67***	0.47
Asian-American	−1.23	0.93	−1.06	0.90	−1.40	0.90	−2.51**	0.85
Latino/a	−6.57***	0.52	−4.00***	0.51	−6.09***	0.51	−5.81***	0.48
Control variables								
Sex (female)	−0.80**	0.29	−0.87**	0.29	−1.76***	0.29	−3.37***	0.27
Age (years)	6.34***	0.42	6.55***	0.42	6.27***	0.40	3.78***	0.39
Non-Mexican immigrant family	−0.67	0.60	−1.46**	0.60	−0.89	0.58	−0.66	0.55
West[a]	−	−	−	−	−	−	−	−
South	−0.20	0.76	0.54	0.69	−0.02	0.62	0.53	0.71
Midwest	0.19	0.82	−0.01	0.74	−0.14	0.77	−0.01	0.76
Northeast	−1.12	0.85	−1.55*	0.77	−1.53+	0.81	−1.45+	0.79
Small town/rural[a]	−	−	−	−	−	−	−	−
Large city	2.30**	0.78	1.44*	0.70	2.49***	0.74	2.20**	0.73
City fringe/ large town	4.81***	0.78	2.87***	0.70	4.69***	0.73	3.95***	0.73
Family socioeconomic factors								
Socioeconomic status	−	−	5.55***	0.24	−	−	−	−
Family poverty status	−	−	−0.63	0.46	−	−	−	−
Family structure (two-parent)	−	−	0.55	0.47	−	−	−	−
Mother not working[a]	−	−	−	−	−	−	−	−
Mother working full-time	−	−	−0.12	0.34	−	−	−	−
Mother working part-time	−	−	0.67	0.40	−	−	−	−
No mother present	−	−	−2.33+	1.29	−	−	−	−
Father not working[a]	−	−	−	−	−	−	−	−

	Model 5		Model 6		Model 7		Model 8	
	b	SE	b	SE	b	SE	b	SE
Race/ethnicity and immigration status								
Mexican immigrant family	−0.68	0.70	−7.62***	0.97	−8.68***	0.79	−8.68***	0.82
White[a]	−	−	−	−	−	−	−	−
African-American	−4.56***	0.38	−6.84***	0.51	−9.03***	0.51	−8.30***	0.55
Asian-American	−2.12*	0.69	−1.00	0.92	−1.06	0.92	−1.05	0.93
Latino/a	−1.45***	0.40	−3.98***	0.55	−6.01***	0.52	−5.79***	0.52
Control variables								
Sex (female)	−0.94***	0.22	−1.16***	0.73	−0.75*	0.29	−0.91**	0.29
Age (years)	−0.71*	0.32	6.59***	0.79	6.40***	0.41	5.92***	0.41
Non-Mexican immigrant family	−0.16	0.45	−1.16+	0.82	−0.74	0.59	−0.72	0.59
West[a]	−	−	−	−	−	−	−	−
South	−0.03	0.55	0.59	0.75	0.23	0.75	0.27	0.75
Midwest	−0.40	0.59	0.05	0.75	−0.06	0.80	0.50	0.83
Northeast	−2.46***	0.61	−1.35+	0.82	−1.20	0.84	−1.12	0.85
Small town/rural[a]	−	−	−	−	−	−	−	−
Large city	0.56	0.56	1.33+	0.75	1.79*	0.77	2.91***	0.80
City fringe/ large town	0.95+	0.56	2.71***	0.75	4.12***	0.77	4.02***	0.77
Cognitive factors								
Low English-language proficiency	−1.98**	0.72	−	−	−	−	−	−
Kindergarten math score	1.22***	0.01	−	−	−	−	−	−
Family factors								
Family non-English-language use	−	−	−0.24	0.27	−	−	−	−
Home learning activities	−	−	−0.16	0.31	−	−	−	−
Home reading activities	−	−	1.00***	0.22	−	−	−	−
Parental involvement in education	−	−	1.47***	0.10	−	−	−	−

(*continued*)

Table A12 *Continued*

	Model 1		Model 2		Model 3		Model 4	
	b	SE	b	SE	b	SE	b	SE
Family socioeconomic factors (continued)								
Father working full-time	–	–	2.72***	0.77	–	–	–	–
Father working part-time	–	–	3.79***	1.13	–	–	–	–
No father present	–	–	1.85*	0.87	–	–	–	–
Health factors[b]								
Poor general health	–	–	–	–	–1.07***	0.18	–	–
Physical health problems	–	–	–	–	–1.13***	0.24	–	–
Internalizing symptoms	–	–	–	–	–4.37***	0.30	–	–
Externalizing symptoms	–	–	–	–	–2.30***	0.24	–	–
Psychosocial factors								
Self-regulation	–	–	–	–	–	–	10.40***	0.30
Social competence	–	–	–	–	–	–	–2.00***	0.31
Intercept	17.02***	2.74	12.83***	2.77	25.04***	2.96	8.68***	2.58
δ *2 Res LL (vs. Model 1)*	–		–739		–601		–1645	

n = 9,637 (all models).

*** $p < 0.001$.

** $p < 0.01$.

* $p < 0.05$.

+ $p = 0.10$.

[a] Reference category for set of dummy variables. The employment and child care dummy variables also include a binary marker for those missing employment information.

[b] A special set of three control variables (health care and coverage, parental physical health, parental depression) were included in models in which the health factors were examined because they were included in the health models in Chapter 3.

[c] A special set of control variables (teacher race/ethnicity, school language services, school sector) were included in models in which the school factors were examined.

	Model 5		Model 6		Model 7		Model 8	
	b	SE	b	SE	b	SE	b	SE
Child care factors								
Parental care only[a]	–	–	–	–	–	–	–	–
Preschool	–	–	–	–	3.79***	0.44	–	–
Day care	–	–	–	–	2.94***	0.62	–	–
Home-based care	–	–	–	–	1.37**	0.46	–	–
Other child care arrangement	–	–	–	–	−1.43**	0.53	–	–
School factors[c]								
School size	–	–	–	–	–	–	0.29	0.27
Low teacher experience	–	–	–	–	–	–	−0.16	0.11
Minority representation	–	–	–	–	–	–	−0.03**	0.01
Proportion of students in poverty	–	–	–	–	–	–	−9.66***	1.19
Disorganized community location	–	–	–	–	–	–	−0.18	0.39
Safety problems in school	–	–	–	–	–	–	−0.76*	0.39
Intercept	34.76***	2.04	8.32**	2.90	15.21***	2.75	22.84***	3.04
δ *2 Res LL (vs. Model 1)*	−5642		−251		−155		−276	

Table A13 Results of Comprehensive Regression Model Predicting Math Achievement in First Grade by All Six Developmental Domains and Contexts

	Model 9	
	b	*SE*
Race/ethnicity and immigration status		
Mexican immigrant family	−1.59*	0.78
White[a]	−	−
African-American	−3.24***	0.41
Asian-American	−2.47***	0.68
Latino/a	−1.44***	0.42
Control variables		
Sex (female)	−1.95***	0.23
Age (years)	−0.94**	0.32
Non-Mexican immigrant family	−0.61	0.46
West[a]	−	−
South	0.48	0.54
Midwest	−0.33	0.60
Northeast	−2.23***	0.62
Small town/rural[a]	−	−
Large city	0.63	0.58
City fringe/large town	0.42	0.56
Family socioeconomic factors		
Socioeconomic status	1.19***	0.19
Family poverty status	0.60	0.35
Family structure (two-parent)	0.89*	0.36
Mother not working[a]	−	−
Mother working full-time	0.14	0.27
Mother working part-time	0.14	0.31
No mother present	−2.11*	0.98
Father not working[a]	−	−
Father working full-time	1.11[+]	0.58
Father working part-time	1.85*	0.85
No father present	0.65	0.66
Health factors[b]		
Poor general health	−0.40**	0.14
Physical health problems	−0.29[+]	0.18
Internalizing symptoms	−0.99***	0.23
Externalizing symptoms	−0.30	0.20

	Model 9	
	b	*SE*
Psychosocial factors		
Self-regulation	3.72***	0.25
Social competence	−0.92***	0.26
Cognitive factors		
Low English-language proficiency	−2.16**	0.73
Kindergarten math score	1.06***	0.01
Family factors		
Family non-English-language use	0.46*	0.20
Home learning activities	−0.29	0.23
Home reading activities	0.27+	0.16
Parental involvement in education	0.36***	0.08
Child care factors		
Parental care only[a]	−	−
Preschool	−0.43	0.33
Day care	−0.20	0.47
Home-based care	0.42	0.36
Other child care arrangement	−1.29***	0.40
School factors[b]		
School size	0.26	0.19
Low teacher experience	−0.14	0.08
Minority representation	−0.02*	0.00
Proportion of students in poverty	−2.04*	0.89
Disorganized community location	0.38	0.28
Safety problems in school	−0.32	0.29
Intercept	31.97***	2.77
δ *2 Res LL (vs. Model 1 in Table A12)*	−6294	

n = 9,637 (all models).
*** *p* < 0.001.
** *p* < 0.01.
* *p* < 0.05.
+ *p* < 0.10.

[a] Reference category for set of dummy variables. The employment and child care dummy variables also include a binary marker for those missing employment or child care information.

[b] A special set of three control variables (health care and coverage, parental physical health, parental depression) was included in models in which the health factors were examined because they were included in the health models in Chapter 3, and a special set of control variables (teacher race or ethnicity, school language services, school sector) was included in models in which the school factors were examined.

Table A14 Results of Regression Models Predicting Growth in Math Achievement Between First and Third Grade by Various Developmental Domains and Contexts

	Model 1		Model 2		Model 3		Model 4	
	b	SE	b	SE	b	SE	b	SE
First-grade math score	0.84***	0.01	0.81***	0.01	0.82***	0.01	0.78***	0.01
Race/ethnicity and immigration status								
Mexican immigrant family	−3.34***	0.58	−1.69**	0.60	−1.73**	0.60	−2.23***	0.58
White[a]	−	−	−	−	−	−	−	−
African-American	−4.36***	0.38	−3.67***	0.39	−3.61***	0.39	−3.71***	0.39
Asian-American	0.29	0.68	0.40	0.68	0.33	0.68	−0.12	0.67
Latino/a	−0.86*	0.38	0.09	0.39	−0.16	0.39	−0.29	0.38
Control variables								
Sex (female)	−2.23***	0.21	−2.27***	0.21	−2.52***	0.22	−3.19***	0.22
Age (years)	−2.09***	0.31	−1.83***	0.31	−1.81***	0.31	−2.42***	0.31
Non-Mexican immigrant family	2.01***	0.44	1.71***	0.44	1.67***	0.43	1.73***	0.43
West[a]	−	−	−	−	−	−	−	−
South	−0.20	0.55	0.07	0.54	0.06	0.53	0.28	0.53
Midwest	0.40	0.59	0.33	0.57	0.27	0.57	0.29	0.57
Northeast	0.43	0.61	0.28	0.60	0.18	0.60	0.12	0.60
Small town/rural[a]	−	−	−	−	−	−	−	−
Large city	0.93+	0.56	0.63	0.55	0.72	0.55	0.73	0.54
City fringe/large town	1.58**	0.56	0.94+	0.55	1.05+	0.55	0.96+	0.55
Family socioeconomic factors								
Socioeconomic status	−	−	1.87***	0.19	−	−	−	−
Family poverty status	−	−	−1.10**	0.35	−	−	−	−
Family structure (two-parent)	−	−	0.39	0.35	−	−	−	−
Mother not working[a]	−	−	−	−	−	−	−	−
Mother working full-time	−	−	0.06	0.26	−	−	−	−
Mother working part-time	−	−	0.43	0.30	−	−	−	−
No mother present	−	−	−0.01	0.98	−	−	−	−
Father not working[a]	−	−	−	−	−	−	−	−

	Model 5		Model 6		Model 7		Model 8	
	b	SE	b	SE	b	SE	b	SE
First-grade math score	0.68***	0.01	0.83***	0.01	0.83***	0.01	0.83***	0.01
Race/ethnicity and immigration status								
Mexican immigrant family	−0.77	0.68	−1.73*	0.73	−1.60**	0.60	−1.42*	0.62
White[a]	−	−	−	−	−	−	−	−
African-American	−3.60***	0.38	−3.63***	0.39	−3.62***	0.39	−3.28***	0.41
Asian-American	−0.05	0.66	0.42	0.68	0.42	0.68	0.49	0.68
Latino/a	0.38	0.38	−0.10	0.41	−0.04	0.39	0.12	0.40
Control variables								
Sex (female)	−2.42***	0.21	−2.40***	0.22	−2.27***	0.21	−2.26***	0.21
Age (years)	−3.30***	0.31	−1.81***	0.31	−1.80***	0.31	−1.92***	0.31
Non-Mexican immigrant family	1.86***	0.43	1.75***	0.46	1.72***	0.44	1.67***	0.44
West[a]	−	−	−	−	−	−	−	−
South	0.02	0.52	0.09	0.54	0.05	0.53	−0.06	0.54
Midwest	0.19	0.56	0.35	0.58	0.32	0.57	0.30	0.60
Northeast	−0.26	0.59	0.24	0.60	0.27	0.60	0.30	0.62
Small town/rural[a]	−	−	−	−	−	−	−	−
Large city	0.45	0.54	0.59	0.55	0.61	0.55	1.26*	0.58
City fringe/large town	0.53	0.54	0.89+	0.55	0.92+	0.55	0.94+	0.56
Cognitive factors								
Low English-language proficiency	−0.14	0.69	−	−	−	−	−	−
Kindergarten math score	0.40***	0.02	−	−	−	−	−	−
Family factors								
Family non-English-language use	−	−	0.06	0.20	−	−	−	−
Home learning activities	−	−	0.39+	0.23	−	−	−	−
Home reading activities	−	−	0.32*	0.16	−	−	−	−
Parental involvement in education	−	−	0.24**	0.08	−	−	−	−

(continued)

Table A14 *Continued*

	Model 1		Model 2		Model 3		Model 4	
	b	*SE*	*b*	*SE*	*b*	*SE*	*b*	*SE*
Family socioeconomic factors (continued)								
Father working full-time	–	–	0.81	0.58	–	–	–	–
Father working part-time	–	–	0.71	0.85	–	–	–	–
No father present	–	–	1.43*	0.66	–	–	–	–
Health factors[b]								
Poor general health	–	–	–	–	−0.24[+]	0.14	–	–
Physical health problems	–	–	–	–	−0.05	0.18	–	–
Internalizing symptoms	–	–	–	–	−1.26***	0.23	–	–
Externalizing symptoms	–	–	–	–	−0.57**	0.19	–	–
Psychosocial factors								
Self-regulation	–	–	–	–	–	–	3.65***	0.25
Social competence	–	–	–	–	–	–	−0.85***	0.25
Intercept	52.33***	2.01	51.10***	2.10	54.62***	2.24	50.39***	2.02
δ *2 Res LL (vs. Model 1)*	–		−170		−90		−310	

$n = 9{,}637$ (all models).

*** $p < 0.001$.

** $p < 0.01$.

* $p < 0.05$.

[+] $p = 0.10$.

[a] Reference category for set of dummy variables. The employment and child care dummy variables also include a binary marker for those missing employment or child care information.

[b] A special set of three control variables (health care and coverage, parental physical health, parental depression) were included in models in which the health factors were examined because they were included in the health models in Chapter 3.

[c] A special set of control variables (teacher race or ethnicity, school language services, school sector) were included in models in which the school factors were examined.

	Model 5		Model 6		Model 7		Model 8	
	b	*SE*	*b*	*SE*	*b*	*SE*	*b*	*SE*
Child care factors								
Parental care only[a]	–	–	–	–	–	–	–	–
Preschool	–	–	–	–	0.39	0.33	–	–
Day care	–	–	–	–	0.77[+]	0.47	–	–
Home-based care	–	–	–	–	0.39	0.36	–	–
Other child care arrangement	–	–	–	–	−0.08	0.40	–	–
School factors[c]								
School size	–	–	–	–	–	–	0.12	0.19
Low teacher experience	–	–	–	–	–	–	0.03	0.08
Minority representation	–	–	–	–	–	–	−0.02*	0.00
Proportion of students in poverty	–	–	–	–	–	–	−3.36***	0.89
Disorganized community location	–	–	–	–	–	–	0.14	0.28
Safety problems in school	–	–	–	–	–	–	−0.26	0.28
Intercept	61.22***	1.98	50.58***	2.15	51.51***	2.03	53.92***	2.25
δ *2 Res LL (vs. Model 1)*	−552		−38		−29		−59	

Table A15 Results of Comprehensive Regression Model Predicting Growth in Math Achievement Between First and Third Grade by All Six Developmental Domains and Contexts

	Model 9	
	b	*SE*
First-grade math score	0.64***	0.01
Race/ethnicity and immigration status		
Mexican immigrant family	−1.28[+]	0.75
White[a]	−	−
African-American	-3.10***	0.40
Asian-American	−0.32	0.66
Latino/a	0.30	0.41
Control variables		
Sex (female)	−3.18***	0.22
Age (years)	−3.65***	0.31
Non-Mexican immigrant family	1.71***	0.45
West[a]	−	−
South	0.01	0.53
Midwest	0.03	0.58
Northeast	−0.34	0.60
Small town/rural[a]	−	−
Large city	1.21*	0.56
City fringe/large town	0.61	0.55
Family socioeconomic factors		
Socioeconomic status	1.09***	0.19
Family poverty status	−0.56	0.34
Family structure (two-parent)	−0.17	0.34
Mother not working[a]	−	−
Mother working full-time	−0.01	0.27
Mother working part-time	0.28	0.28
No mother present	−0.15	0.95
Father not working[a]	−	−
Father working full-time	0.51	0.56
Father working part-time	0.64	0.82
No father present	1.22[+]	0.64
Health factors[b]		
Poor general health	−0.22[+]	0.13
Physical health problems	−0.08	0.17
Internalizing symptoms	−0.60**	0.22

Table A15 *Continued*

	Model 9	
	b	*SE*
Health factors[b] (continued)		
Externalizing symptoms	−0.08	0.19
Psychosocial factors		
Self-regulation	2.87***	0.25
Social competence	−0.74***	0.25
Cognitive factors		
Low English-language proficiency	−0.34	0.70
Kindergarten math score	0.36***	0.02
Family factors		
Family non-English-language use	0.18	0.20
Home learning activities	0.53*	0.22
Home reading activities	0.05	0.16
Parental involvement in education	0.19*	0.08
Child care factors		
Parental care only[a]	−	−
Preschool	−0.21	0.32
Day care	0.22	0.46
Home-based care	0.09	0.35
Other child care arrangement	−0.28	0.39
School factors[b]		
School size	0.17	0.19
Low teacher experience	0.01	0.08
Minority representation	−0.02**	0.00
Proportion of students in poverty	−3.07***	0.87
Disorganized community location	0.25	0.27
Safety problems in school	−0.30	0.28
Intercept	59.57***	2.71
δ 2 Res LL (vs. Model 1 in Table A14)	−893	

n = 9,637 (all models).

*** *p* < 0.001.

** *p* < 0.01.

* *p* < 0.05.

+ *p* < 0.10.

[a] Reference category for set of dummy variables. The employment and child care dummy variables also included a binary marker for those missing employment or child care information.

[b] A special set of three control variables (health care and coverage, parental physical health, parental depression) was included in models in which the health factors were examined because they were included in the health models in Chapter 3, and a special set of control variables (teacher race or ethnicity, school language services, school sector) was included in models in which the school factors were examined.

Notes

Chapter 1

1. U.S. Department of Immigration Statistics, 2005.
2. Hirschman, 2001; Wilson, 1991.
3. Adelman, 1999; Schneider & Stevenson, 1999.
4. Suarez-Orozco & Suarez-Orozco, 1995.
5. Entwisle & Alexander, 2002.
6. Coleman, 1990; Millstein, 1988.
7. Bean & Stevens, 2003.
8. Morgan, 2001; Coleman, 1990.
9. See Pianta & Cox, 1999.
10. Alexander & Entwisle, 1988; Entwisle & Alexander, 2002.
11. Adelman, 1999; Stevenson et al., 1994.
12. Hernandez, 2004; Harris, 1999; Kao & Tienda, 1995.
13. Sewell & Hauser, 1980.

Chapter 2

1. Rumbaut, 2004.
2. Hernandez, 2004; Alba & Nee, 2003; Hirschman, 2001; Alba, 1990.
3. Rumbaut, 2004; Kao & Tienda, 1995.
4. Bean & Stevens, 2003.
5. Portes & Zhou, 1993.
6. Hernandez, 2004; Bean & Stevens, 2003; Portes & Rumbaut, 2001.
7. Portes & Rumbaut, 2001.
8. Crosnoe et al., 2004; Kao, 1999.
9. Valenzuela, 1999; Matute-Bianchi, 1986.
10. Denton & West, 2002.

Chapter 3

1. Raver & Zigler, 1997.
2. Currie, 2005; Needham et al., 2004; Thies, 1999; National Education and Health Consortium, 1992; Hagen & Kamberelis, 1990.
3. Berrueta-Clement et al., 1984.
4. Needham et al., 2004; Gutman et al., 2003; Field et al., 2001; Roeser & Eccles, 2000; Dishion et al., 1995; Nolen-Hoeksema et al., 1986.
5. Hernandez, 2004; Harris, 1999; Frisbie et al., 1998.
6. Hernandez, 2004; Mendoza & Dixon, 1999; Arcia, 1998.
7. Takanishi, 2004; Mendoza & Dixon, 1999; Harris, 1999; Mendoza, 1994.
8. Ferraro & Farmer, 1999.
9. Harker, 2001.
10. Valenzuela, 1999; Matute-Bianchi, 1986.
11. Roeser & Eccles, 2000.
12. Crosnoe, 2006.
13. Farkas, 1996.
14. Raver, 2002; Alexander et al., 1993.
15. McClelland et al., 2000; Cooper & Farran, 1988.
16. Raver, 2002; Alexander et al., 1993; Foulkes & Morrow, 1989.
17. Raver & Zigler, 1997; Huston et al., 1994; Parke & Ladd, 1992.
18. Birch & Ladd, 1998; Pianta & Steinberg, 1992.
19. Ladd et al., 1996; Cohen, 1982.
20. Valenzuela, 1999; Matute-Bianchi, 1986.
21. Portes & Rumbaut, 2001; Suarez-Orozco & Suarez-Orozco, 2001.
22. Crosnoe & Lopez-Gonzalez, 2005; Zhou, 1997.
23. Alba et al., 2002; Meouw & Xie, 1999; Igoa, 1995.
24. Lee & Burkham, 2002; Alexander & Entwisle, 1988; Ginsburg, 1989; Heyns, 1978.
25. Hill, 2004; Gandara et al., 2003.
26. Lee & Burkham, 2002; Denton & West, 2002.

Chapter 4

1. Steinberg, 2001.
2. Brooks-Gunn & Markman, 2005; Pianta & Walsh, 1996.
3. Stanton-Salazar, 2001; Suarez-Orozco & Suarez-Orozco, 1995; Valenzuela & Dornbusch, 1994.
4. Call & Mortimer, 2001.
5. Brooks-Gunn & Markman, 2005; Coleman, 1990.
6. Magnuson et al., 2004; Eccles & Harold, 1993; Coleman, 1990.
7. Crosnoe, 2001.

8. Hill, 2004; Suarez-Orozco & Suarez-Orozco, 2001; Valenzuela, 1999.

9. Brooks-Gunn & Markman, 2005; Meouw & Xie, 1999; Igoa, 1995.

10. Hill, 2004; Gandara et al., 2003.

11. Yoshikawa, 2005; Suarez-Orozco & Suarez-Orozco, 2001.

12. Suarez-Orozco & Suarez-Orozco, 1995.

13. Brooks-Gunn & Markman, 2005; Lee & Burkham, 2002.

14. Suarez-Orozco & Suarez-Orozco, 1995.

15. Schneider & Coleman, 1993.

16. Lareau, 2004; Schneider & Coleman, 1993.

17. Lopez et al., 1995; Stanton-Salazar & Dornbusch, 1995; Keith & Lichtman et al., 1992.

18. Pianta & Cox, 1999.

19. Hofferth et al., 1998.

20. Takanishi, 2004; Scarr, 1998.

21. Magnuson et al., 2004; Scarr, 1998; Clarke-Stewart et al., 1994.

22. NICHD Early Child Care Research Network, 1998, 2002; Scarr, 1998.

23. Belsky, 1999; NICHD Early Child Care Research Network, 1998.

24. Igoa, 1995.

25. Magnuson et al., 2004; Takanishi, 2004; Suarez-Orozco & Suarez-Orozco, 2001.

26. Brandon, 2004.

27. Kozol, 1991.

28. Roscigno, 1998; Lee & Smith, 1997; McNeal, 1997; Bryk et al., 1993.

29. For example, Suarez-Orozco & Suarez-Orozco, 2001; Valencia, 2000; Valenzuela, 1999; Matute-Bianchi, 1986.

30. Crosnoe, 2005.

31. Lee & Burkham, 2002.

32. Lee & Smith, 1997.

Chapter 5

1. Schneider et al., 1998.

Chapter 7

1. Hernandez, 2004.

2. NICHD Early Child Care Research Network, 2002.

3. See Kirst, 1994.

Appendix

1. Denton & West, 2002.

2. Lee & Burkham, 2002.

3. http://nces.ed.gov/ecls

4. U.S. Bureau of the Census, 1999.

5. Denton & West, 2002.

6. See Denton & West, 2002.

7. See Duncan & De Avila, 1998.

8. Lee & Burkham, 2002.

9. Ferraro & Farmer, 1999.

10. See Harris, 1999.

11. Centers for Disease Control and Prevention, 2002.

12. Roeser & Eccles, 2000.

13. Crosnoe, 2005.

14. Radloff & Locke, 1986.

15. See Magnuson and colleagues' (2004) article in *American Educational Research Journal.*

16. Lee & Burkham, 2002.

17. Singer, 1998.

18. Currie, 2005.

19. Morgan, 2001; Heckman et al., 1997.

20. Becker & Ichino, 2002.

21. Becker & Ichino, 2002.

References

Adelman, C. (1999). *Answers in the toolbox: Academic intensity, attendance patterns, and bachelor's degree attainment.* U.S. Department of Education, Office of Educational Research and Improvement. Washington, DC: U.S. Government Printing Office.

Alba, R. D. (1990). *Ethnic identity: The transformation of white America.* New Haven, CT: Yale University Press.

Alba, R. [D.], Logan, J., Lutz, A., & Stults, B. (2002). Only English by the third generation? Loss and preservation of the mother tongue among the grandchildren of contemporary immigrants. *Demography, 39,* 467–484.

Alba, R. D., & Nee, V. (2003). *Remaking the American mainstream: Assimilation and contemporary immigration.* Cambridge, MA: Harvard University Press.

Alexander, K. L., & Entwisle, D. R. (1988). Achievement in the first two years of school: Patterns and processes. *Monographs of the Society for Research in Child Development, 53,* 1–157.

Alexander, K. L., Entwisle, D. R., & Dauber, S. L. (1993). First grade classroom behavior: Its short- and long-term consequences for school performance. *Child Development, 64,* 801–814.

Arcia, E. (1998). Latino perceptions of their children's health status. *Social Science and Medicine, 46,* 1271–1274.

Bean, F., & Stevens, G. (2003). *America's newcomers and the dynamics of diversity.* New York: Russell Sage.

Becker, S. O., & Ichino, A. (2002). Estimation of average treatment effects based on propensity scores. *Stata Journal, 2,* 358–377.

Belsky, J. (1999). Developmental risks still associated with early child care. *Journal of Child Psychology and Psychiatry, 42,* 845–859.

Berrueta-Clement, J. R., Schweinhart, L. J., Barnett, W. S., Epstein, A. S., & Wiekart, D. P. (1984). *Changed lives: The effects of the Perry Preschool Program on youths through age 19.* Ypsilanti, MI: High/Scope Press.

Birch, S. H., & Ladd, G. W. (1998). Children's interpersonal behaviors and the teacher-child relationship. *Developmental Psychology, 34,* 934–946.

Brandon, P. (2004). The child care arrangements of preschool-age children in immigrant families in the United States. *International Migration, 42,* 65–87.

Brooks-Gunn, J., & Markman, L. B. (2005). The contribution of parenting to ethnic and racial gaps in school readiness. *Future of Children, 15,* 139–168.

Bryk, A. S., Lee, V. E., & Holland, P. B. (1993). *Catholic schools and the common good.* Cambridge, MA: Harvard University Press.

Call, K. T., & Mortimer, J. T. (2001). *Arenas of comfort in adolescence: A study of adjustment in context.* Mahwah, NJ: Erlbaum.

Centers for Disease Control and Prevention. 2002. *Body mass index.* Available at http://www.cdc.gov/nccdphp/dnpa/bmi

Clarke-Stewart, A., Gruber, C., & Fitzgerald, L. M. (1994). *Children at home and in day care.* Hillsdale, NJ: Erlbaum.

Cohen, E. G. (1982). Expectation states and interracial interaction in school settings. *Annual Review of Sociology, 8,* 209–235.

Coleman, J. (1990). *Foundations of social theory.* Cambridge, MA: Harvard University Press.

Cooper, D. H., & Farran, D. C. (1988). Behavioral risk factors in kindergarten. *Early Childhood Research Quarterly, 3,* 1–19.

Crosnoe, R. (2001). Academic orientation and parental involvement in education during high school. *Sociology of Education, 74,* 210–230.

Crosnoe, R. (2005). Double disadvantage or signs of resilience: The elementary school contexts of children from Mexican immigrant families. *American Educational Research Journal, 42,* 269–303.

Crosnoe, R. (2006). Health and the education of children from race/ethnic minority and immigrant families. *Journal of Health and Social Behavior, 47,* 77–93.

Crosnoe, R., & Lopez-Gonzalez, L. (2005). Immigration from Mexico, school composition, and adolescent functioning. *Sociological Perspectives, 48,* 1–24.

Crosnoe, R., Lopez-Gonzalez, L., & Muller, C. (2004). Immigration from Mexico into the math/science pipeline in American education. *Social Science Quarterly, 85,* 1208–1226.

Currie, J. (2005). Health disparities and gaps in school readiness. *Future of Children, 15,* 117–138.

Denton, K., & West, J. (2002). *Children's reading and mathematics achievement in kindergarten and first grade.* Washington, DC: U.S. Department of Education.

Dishion, T. J., French, D. C., & Patterson, G. R. (1995). The development and ecology of antisocial behavior. In D. Cicchetti & D. J. Cohen (Eds.), *Developmental psychopathology: Risk, disorder, and adaptation* (pp. 421–471). New York: Wiley.

Duncan, S. E., & De Avila, E. (1998). *PreLAS 2000 Cue Picture Book English Form C.* Monterey, CA: CTB/McGraw-Hill.

Eccles, J. S., & Harold, R. D. (1993). Parent-school involvement during the early adolescent years. *Teachers College Record, 94*(3), 568–587.

Entwisle, D. R., & Alexander, K. L. (2002). The first grade transition in life course perspective. In J. Mortimer & M. Shanahan (Eds.), *Handbook of the life course* (pp. 229–250). New York: Kluwer Academic/Plenum.

Farkas, G. (1996). *Human capital or cultural capital? Ethnicity and poverty groups in an urban school district.* New York: Aldine de Gruyter.

Ferraro, K. F., & Farmer, M. F. (1999). Utility of health data from social surveys: Is there a gold standard for measuring morbidity? *American Sociological Review, 64*, 303–315.

Field, T., Diego, D., & Sanders, C. (2001). Adolescent depression and risk factors. *Adolescence, 36*, 491–498.

Foulkes, B., & Morrow, R. D. (1989). Academic survival skills for the young child at risk for school failure. *Journal of Educational Research, 82*, 158–165.

Frisbie, W. P., Forbes, D., & Hummer, R. A. (1998). Hispanic pregnancy outcomes: Additional evidence. *Social Science Quarterly, 79*, 149–169.

Gandara, P., Rumberger, R., Maxwell-Jolly, J., & Callahan, R. (2003). English learners in California schools: Unequal resources, unequal outcomes. *Education Policy Analysis Archives, 11*(36). Available at http://epaa.asu.edu/epaa/v11n36/

Ginsburg, H. P. (1989). *Children's arithmetic: How they learn it and how you teach it.* Austin, TX: Pro Ed.

Gutman, L., Sameroff, A. J., & Cole, R. (2003). Academic growth curve trajectories from first grade to twelfth grade: Effects of multiple social risk factors and preschool child factors. *Developmental Psychology, 39*, 777–790.

Hagen, J. W., & Kamberelis, G. (1990). Cognition and academic performance in children with learning disabilities, low academic achievement, diabetes mellitus, and seizure disorders. In H. L. Swanson & B. K. Keogh (Eds.), *Learning disabilities: Theoretical and research issues* (pp. 299–314). Hillsdale, NJ: Erlbaum.

Harker, K. (2001). Immigrant generation, assimilation, and adolescent psychological well-being. *Social Forces, 79*, 969–1004.

Harris, K. M. (1999). The health status and risk behaviors of adolescents in immigrant families. In D. J. Hernandez (Ed.), *Children of immigrants: Health, adjustment, and public assistance* (pp. 286–347). Washington, DC: National Academy Press.

Heckman, J. J., Ichimura, H., & Todd, P. (1997). Matching as an econometric evaluation estimator: Evidence from evaluating a job training programme. *Review of Economic Studies, 64*, 605–654.

Hernandez, D. J. (2004). Demographic change and the life circumstances of immigrant families. *Future of Children, 14*, 17–48.

Heyns, B. (1978). *Summer learning and the effects of schooling.* New York: Academic Press.

Hill, E. G. (2004). *A look at the progress of English learner students.* Sacramento, CA: Legislative Analyst's Office.

Hirschman, C. (2001). The educational enrollment of immigrant youth: A test of the segmented-assimilation hypothesis. *Demography, 38*, 317–336.

Hofferth, S. L., Akin, K., Henke, R., & West, J. (1998). *Characteristics of children's early care and education programs: Data from the 1995 National Household Education Survey.* Washington, DC: National Center for Education Statistics.

Huston, A. C., McLoyd, V., & Garcia-Coll, C. (1994). Children and poverty: Issues in contemporary research. *Child Development, 65*, 275–282.

Igoa, C. (1995). *The inner world of the immigrant child.* New York: St. Martin's Press.

Kao, G. (1999). Psychological well-being and educational achievement among immigrant youth. In D. J. Hernandez (Ed.), *Children of immigrants: Health, adjustment, and public assistance* (pp. 410–477). Washington, DC: National Academy Press.

Kao, G., & Tienda, M. (1995). Optimism and achievement: The educational performance of immigrant youth. *Social Science Quarterly, 76*, 1–19.

Keith, P., & Lichtman, M. (1992). *Testing the influences of parental involvement on Mexican-American eighth grade students' academic achievement.* Paper presented at the annual meeting of the American Educational Research Association, San Francisco, California (ERIC Document Reproduction Service no. ED 351 170).

Kirst, M. (1994). Equity for children: Linking education and children's services. *Educational Policy, 8*, 583–590.

Kozol, J. (1991). *Savage inequalities.* New York: Crown.

Ladd, G. W., Kochenderfer, R. J., & Coleman, C. C. (1996). Friendship quality as a predictor of young children's early school adjustment. *Child Development, 67*, 1102–1118.

Lareau, A. (2004). *Unequal childhoods: Class, race, and family life.* Berkeley: University of California Press.

Lee, V., & Burkham, D. (2002). *Inequality at the starting gate: Social background differences in achievement as children begin school.* Washington, DC: Economic Policy Institute.

Lee, V. E., & Smith, J. B. (1997). High school size: Which works best and for whom? *Educational Evaluation and Policy Analysis, 19*, 205–227.

Lopez, L. C., Rodriguez, R. F., & Sanchez, V. (1995). The relationships between parental education and school involvement of Mexican-American parents. *Psychological Reports, 77*, 1203–1207.

Magnuson, K. A., Meyers, M. K., Ruhm, C. J., & Waldfogel, J. (2004). Inequality in preschool education and school readiness. *American Educational Research Journal, 41*, 115–158.

Matute-Bianchi, M. E. (1986). Ethnic identities and patterns of school success and failure among Mexican-descent and Japanese-American students in a California high school: An ethnographic analysis. *American Journal of Education, 95,* 233–255.

McClelland, M., Morrison, F., & Holmes, D. (2000). Children at risk for early academic problems: The role of learning-related social skills. *Early Childhood Research Quarterly, 15,* 307–329.

McNeal, R. (1997). High school dropouts: A closer examination of school effects. *Social Science Quarterly, 78,* 209–222.

Mendoza, F. S. (1994). The health of Latino children in the United States. *Future of Children, 4,* 43–72.

Mendoza, F. S., & Dixon, L. B. (1999). The health and nutritional status of immigrant Hispanic children: Analyses of the Hispanic Health and Nutrition Examination Survey. In D. J. Hernandez (Ed.), *Children of immigrants: Health, adjustment, and public assistance* (pp. 187–243). Washington, DC: National Academy Press.

Meouw, T., & Xie, Y. (1999). Bilingualism and the academic achievement of Asian immigrants. *American Sociological Review, 64,* 232–253.

Millstein, S. G. (1988). *The potential of school-linked centers to promote adolescent health and development.* Washington, DC: Carnegie Foundation.

Morgan, S. L. (2001). Counterfactuals, causal effect heterogeneity, and the Catholic school effect on learning. *Sociology of Education, 74,* 341–374.

National Education and Health Consortium. (1992). The relationship of health to learning: Healthy brain development. In H. M. Wallace, K. Patrick, G. S. Parcell, & J. B. Igoe (Eds.), *Principles and practices of student health,* v. 2 (pp. 262–272). Oakland, CA: Third Party.

Needham, B. L., Crosnoe, R., & Muller, C. (2004). Academic failure in secondary school: The inter-related role of physical health problems and educational context. *Social Problems, 51,* 569–586.

NICHD Early Child Care Research Network. (1998). Early child care and self-control, compliance, and problem behavior at 24 and 36 months. *Child Development, 69,* 1145–1170.

NICHD Early Child Care Research Network. (2002). Child care and children's development prior to school entry: Results from the NICHD Study of Early Child Care. *American Educational Research Journal, 39,* 133–164.

Nolen-Hoeksema, S., Girgus, J. S., & Seligman, M. E. P. (1986). Learned helplessness in children: A longitudinal study of depression, achievement, and explanatory style. *Journal of Personality and Social Psychology, 51,* 435–442.

Parke, R. D., & Ladd, G. W. (1992). *Family-peer relationships: Modes of linkage.* Hillsdale, NJ: Erlbaum.

Pianta, R. C., & Cox, M. J. (1999). *The transition to kindergarten.* Baltimore: Brookes.

Pianta, R. C., & Steinberg, M. (1992). Teacher-child relationships and the process of adjusting to school. *New Directions for Child Development, 57,* 61–80.

Pianta, R. C., & Walsh, D. J. (1996). *High-risk children in schools: Constructing sustaining relationships.* New York: Routledge.

Portes, A., & Rumbaut, R. G. (2001). *Legacies: The story of the immigrant second generation.* Berkeley: University of California Press.

Portes, A., & Zhou, M. (1993). The new second generation: Segmented assimilation and its variants among post-1965 immigrant youth. *Annals of the American Academy of Political and Social Science, 530,* 740–798.

Radloff, L. S., & Locke, B. S. (1986). The community mental health assessment survey and the CES-D scale. In M. M. Weissman, J. K. Meyers, & C. E. Ross (Eds.), *Community surveys of psychiatric disorders* (pp. 177–189). New Brunswick, NJ: Rutgers University Press.

Raver, C. C. (2002). Emotions matter: Making the case for the role of young children's emotional development for early school readiness. *SRCD Social Policy Report, 16,* 1–20. Ann Arbor, MI: Society for Research in Child Development.

Raver, C. C., & Zigler, E. F. (1997). Social competence: An untapped dimension in evaluating Head Start's success. *Early Childhood Research Quarterly, 12,* 363–385.

Roeser, R., & Eccles, J. S. (2000). Schooling and mental health. In A. J. Sameroff, M. Lewis, & S. Miller (Eds.), *Handbook of developmental psychopathology* (pp. 135–156). Dordrecht, Netherlands: Kluwer.

Roscigno, V. (1998). Race and the reproduction of educational disadvantage. *Social Forces, 76,* 1033–1060.

Rumbaut, R. (2004). Ages, life stages, and generational cohorts: Decomposing the immigrant first and second generation in the United States. *International Migration Review, 38,* 1160–1205.

Scarr, S. (1998). American child care today. *American Psychologist, 53,* 95–108.

Schneider, B., & Coleman, J. S. (1993). *Parents, their children, and schools.* Boulder, CO: Westview.

Schneider, B., & Stevenson, D. (1999). *The ambitious generation: America's teenagers, motivated but directionless.* New Haven, CT: Yale University Press.

Schneider, B., Swanson, C. B., & Riegle-Crumb, C. (1998). Opportunities for learning: Course sequences and positional advantages. *Social Psychology of Education, 2,* 25–53.

Sewell, W. H., & Hauser, R. (1980). The Wisconsin longitudinal study of social and psychological factors in aspirations and achievements. In A. C. Kerckhoff (Ed.), *Research in the sociology of education and socialization* (pp. 59–100). Greenwich, CT: JAI.

Singer, J. D. (1998). Using SAS proc mixed to fit multilevel models, hierarchical models, and individual growth models. *Journal of Educational and Behavioral Statistics, 24,* 323–355.

Stanton-Salazar, R. D. (2001). *Manufacturing hope and despair: The school and kin support networks of U.S.-Mexican youth.* New York: Teacher's College.

Stanton-Salazar, R. D., & Dornbusch, S. M. (1995). Social capital and the reproduction of inequality: Information networks among Mexican-origin high school students. *Sociology of Education, 68,* 116–135.

Steinberg, L. D. (2001). We know some things: Parent-adolescent relationships in retrospect and prospect. *Journal of Research on Adolescence, 11,* 1–20.

Stevenson, D. L., Schiller, K. S., & Schneider, B. (1994). Sequences of opportunities for learning. *Sociology of Education, 67,* 184–198.

Suarez-Orozco, C., & Suarez-Orozco, M. (1995). *Transformations: Immigration, family life, and achievement motivation among Latino adolescents.* Stanford, CA: Stanford University Press.

Suarez-Orozco, C., & Suarez-Orozco, M. (2001). *Children of immigration.* Cambridge, MA: Harvard University Press.

Takanishi, R. (2004). Leveling the playing field: Supporting immigrant children from birth to eight. *Future of Children, 14,* 61–80.

Thies, K. M. (1999). Identifying the educational implications of chronic illness in school children. *Journal of School Health, 69,* 392–397.

U.S. Bureau of the Census. (1999). *Statistical abstract of the United States.* Washington, DC: Author.

U.S. Department of Immigration Statistics. (2005). *Yearbook of immigration statistics.* Washington, DC: Department of Homeland Security.

Valencia, R. (2000). Inequalities and the schooling of minority students in Texas. *Hispanic Journal of Behavioral Sciences, 22,* 445–459.

Valenzuela, A. (1999). *Subtractive schooling: U.S.-Mexican youth and the politics of caring.* Albany, NY: SUNY Press.

Valenzuela, A., & Dornbusch, S. M. (1994). Familism and social capital in the academic achievement of Mexican-origin and Anglo adolescents. *Social Science Quarterly, 75,* 18–36.

Wilson, W. J. (1991). *The truly disadvantaged: The inner-city, the underclass, and public policy.* Chicago: University of Chicago Press.

Yoshikawa, H. (2005). *You can't eat embarrassment.* Paper presented at the biennial meeting of the Society for Research in Child Development, Atlanta, Georgia.

Zhou, M. (1997). Growing up American: The challenge confronting immigrant children and children of immigrants. *Annual Review of Sociology, 23,* 63–95.

Index

Italic page numbers indicate material in figures or tables.